LANGUAGE AND LITERACY SERIES

D1522397

Dorothy S. Strickland, FOUNDING EDITOR
María Paula Ghiso and Donna E. Alvermann, SERIES EDITORS
ADVISORY BOARD: Richard Allington, Kathryn Au, Bernice Cullinan, Colette Daiute,
Anne Haas Dyson, Carole Edelsky, Mary Juzwik, Susan Lytle, Django Paris, Timothy Shanahan

Digitally Supported Disciplinary Literacy for Diverse K–5 Classrooms
JAMIE COLWELL, AMY HUTCHISON, & LINDSAY WOODWARD

The Reading Turn-Around with Emergent Bilinguals: A Five-Part Framework for Powerful Teaching and Learning (Grades K–6)
AMANDA CLAUDIA WAGER, LANE W. CLARKE, & GRACE ENRIQUEZ

Race, Justice, and Activism in Literacy Instruction
VALERIE KINLOCH, TANJA BURKHARD, & CARLOTTA PENN, EDS.

Letting Go of Literary Whiteness: Antiracist Literature Instruction for White Students
CARLIN BORSHEIM-BLACK & SOPHIA TATIANA SARIGIANIDES

The Vulnerable Heart of Literacy: Centering Trauma as Powerful Pedagogy
ELIZABETH DUTRO

Amplifying the Curriculum: Designing Quality Learning Opportunities for English Learners
AÍDA WALQUI & GEORGE C. BUNCH, EDS.

Arts Integration in Diverse K–5 Classrooms: Cultivating Literacy Skills and Conceptual Understanding
LIANE BROUILLETTE

Translanguaging for Emergent Bilinguals: Inclusive Teaching in the Linguistically Diverse Classroom
DANLING FU, XENIA HADJIOANNOU, & XIAODI ZHOU

Before Words: Wordless Picture Books and the Development of Reading in Young Children
JUDITH T. LYSAKER

Seeing the Spectrum: Teaching English Language Arts to Adolescents with Autism
ROBERT ROZEMA

A Think-Aloud Approach to Writing Assessment: Analyzing Process and Product with Adolescent Writers
SARAH W. BECK

"We've Been Doing It Your Way Long Enough": Choosing the Culturally Relevant Classroom
JANICE BAINES, CARMEN TISDALE, & SUSI LONG

Summer Reading: Closing the Rich/Poor Reading Achievement Gap, 2nd Edition
RICHARD L. ALLINGTON & ANNE MCGILL-FRANZEN, EDS.

Educating for Empathy: Literacy Learning and Civic Engagement
NICOLE MIRRA

Preparing English Learners for College and Career: Lessons from Successful High Schools
MARÍA SANTOS ET AL.

Reading the Rainbow: LGBTQ-Inclusive Literacy Instruction in the Elementary Classroom
CAITLIN L. RYAN & JILL M. HERMANN-WILMARTH

Educating Emergent Bilinguals: Policies, Programs, and Practices for English Learners, 2nd Edition
OFELIA GARCÍA & JO ANNE KLEIFGEN

Social Justice Literacies in the English Classroom: Teaching Practice in Action
ASHLEY S. BOYD

Remixing Multiliteracies: Theory and Practice from New London to New Times
FRANK SERAFINI & ELISABETH GEE, EDS.

Culturally Sustaining Pedagogies: Teaching and Learning for Justice in a Changing World
DJANGO PARIS & H. SAMY ALIM, EDS.

Choice and Agency in the Writing Workshop: Developing Engaged Writers, Grades 4–6
FRED L. HAMEL

Assessing Writing, Teaching Writers: Putting the Analytic Writing Continuum to Work in Your Classroom
MARY ANN SMITH & SHERRY SEALE SWAIN

The Teacher-Writer: Creating Writing Groups for Personal and Professional Growth
CHRISTINE M. DAWSON

Every Young Child a Reader: Using Marie Clay's Key Concepts for Classroom Instruction
SHARAN A. GIBSON & BARBARA MOSS

"You Gotta BE the Book": Teaching Engaged and Reflective Reading with Adolescents, 3rd Edition
JEFFREY D. WILHELM

Personal Narrative, Revised: Writing Love and Agency in the High School Classroom
BRONWYN CLARE LAMAY

Inclusive Literacy Teaching: Differentiating Approaches in Multilingual Elementary Classrooms
LORI HELMAN ET AL.

The Vocabulary Book: Learning and Instruction, 2nd Edition
MICHAEL F. GRAVES

Reading, Writing, and Talk: Inclusive Teaching Strategies for Diverse Learners, K–2
MARIANA SOUTO-MANNING & JESSICA MARTELL

Go Be a Writer!: Expanding the Curricular Boundaries of Literacy Learning with Children
CANDACE R. KUBY & TARA GUTSHALL RUCKER

Partnering with Immigrant Communities: Action Through Literacy
GERALD CAMPANO, MARÍA PAULA GHISO, & BETHANY J. WELCH

Teaching Outside the Box but Inside the Standards: Making Room for Dialogue
BOB FECHO, MICHELLE FALTER, & XIAOLI HONG, EDS.

Literacy Leadership in Changing Schools 10 Keys to Successful Professional Development
SHELLEY B. WEPNER ET AL.

continued

For volumes in the NCRLL Collection (edited by JoBeth Allen and Donna E. Alvermann) and the Practitioners Bookshelf Series (edited by Celia Genishi and Donna E. Alvermann), as well as other titles in this series, please visit www.tcpress.com.

Language and Literacy Series, *continued*

Literacy Theory as Practice
LARA J. HANDSFIELD

Literacy and History in Action
THOMAS M. MCCANN ET AL.

Pose, Wobble, Flow
ANTERO GARCIA & CINDY O'DONNELL-ALLEN

Newsworthy—Cultivating Critical Thinkers,
Readers, and Writers in Language Arts Classrooms
ED MADISON

Engaging Writers with Multigenre Research
Projects
NANCY MACK

Teaching Transnational Youth—
Literacy and Education in a Changing World
ALLISON SKERRETT

Uncommonly Good Ideas—
Teaching Writing in the Common Core Era
SANDRA MURPHY & MARY ANN SMITH

The One-on-One Reading and Writing Conference
JENNIFER BERNE & SOPHIE C. DEGENER

Critical Encounters in Secondary English,
3rd Edition
DEBORAH APPLEMAN

Transforming Talk into Text—Argument Writing,
Inquiry, and Discussion, Grades 6–12
THOMAS M. MCCANN

Reading and Representing Across the Content
Areas
AMY ALEXANDRA WILSON & KATHRYN J. CHAVEZ

Writing and Teaching to Change the World
STEPHANIE JONES, ED.

Educating Literacy Teachers Online
LANE W. CLARKE & SUSAN WATTS-TAFFEE

WHAM! Teaching with Graphic Novels Across
the Curriculum
WILLIAM G. BROZO, GARY MOORMAN,
& CARLA K. MEYER

The Administration and Supervision of Reading
Programs, 5th Ed.
SHELLEY B. WEPNER ET AL., EDS.

Critical Literacy in the Early Childhood Classroom
CANDACE R. KUBY

Inspiring Dialogue
MARY M. JUZWIK ET AL.

Reading the Visual
FRANK SERAFINI

Race, Community, and Urban Schools
STUART GREENE

ReWRITING the Basics
ANNE HAAS DYSON

Writing Instruction That Works
ARTHUR N. APPLEBEE ET AL.

Literacy Playshop
KAREN E. WOHLWEND

Critical Media Pedagogy
ERNEST MORRELL ET AL.

A Search Past Silence
DAVID E. KIRKLAND

The ELL Writer
CHRISTINA ORTMEIER-HOOPER

Reading in a Participatory Culture
HENRY JENKINS ET AL., EDS.

Real World Writing for Secondary Students
JESSICA SINGER EARLY & MEREDITH DECOSTA

Teaching Vocabulary to English Language Learners
MICHAEL F. GRAVES ET AL.

Bridging Literacy and Equity
ALTHIER M. LAZAR ET AL.

"Trust Me! I Can Read"
SALLY LAMPING & DEAN WOODRING BLASE

Reading Time
CATHERINE COMPTON-LILLY

The Successful High School Writing Center
DAWN FELS & JENNIFER WELLS, EDS.

Interrupting Hate
MOLLIE V. BLACKBURN

Playing Their Way into Literacies
KAREN E. WOHLWEND

Teaching Literacy for Love and Wisdom
JEFFREY D. WILHELM & BRUCE NOVAK

Urban Literacies
VALERIE KINLOCH, ED.

Bedtime Stories and Book Reports
CATHERINE COMPTON-LILLY & STUART GREENE, EDS.

Envisioning Knowledge
JUDITH A. LANGER

Envisioning Literature, 2nd Edition
JUDITH A. LANGER

Artifactual Literacies
KATE PAHL & JENNIFER ROWSELL

Change Is Gonna Come
PATRICIA A. EDWARDS ET AL.

Harlem on Our Minds
VALERIE KINLOCH

Children, Language, and Literacy
CELIA GENISHI & ANNE HAAS DYSON

Children's Language
JUDITH WELLS LINDFORS

Storytime
LAWRENCE R. SIPE

Digitally Supported Disciplinary Literacy for Diverse K–5 Classrooms

Jamie Colwell
Amy Hutchison
Lindsay Woodward

Foreword by Tom Bean

Teachers College Press

TEACHERS COLLEGE | COLUMBIA UNIVERSITY
NEW YORK AND LONDON

Published by Teachers College Press,® 1234 Amsterdam Avenue, New York, NY 10027

Library of Congress Cataloging-in-Publication Data

Names: Colwell, Jamie, 1981- author. | Hutchison, Amy, 1979– author. | Woodward, Lindsay, author.
Title: Digitally supported disciplinary literacy for diverse K–5 classrooms / Jamie Colwell, Amy Hutchison, Lindsay Woodward.
Description: New York, NY : Teachers College Press, [2020] | Includes bibliographical references and index.
Identifiers: LCCN 2020010031 (print) | LCCN 2020010032 (ebook) | ISBN 9780807764138 (hardcover) | ISBN 9780807764121 (paperback) | ISBN 9780807778685 (ebook)
Subjects: LCSH: Content area reading—Study and teaching (Elementary)—United States. | Content area reading—Computer-assisted instruction. | Language arts (Elementary)—United States. | Language arts (Elementary)—Computer-assisted instruction. | Educational technology—United States.
Classification: LCC LB1050.455 .C64 2020 (print) | LCC LB1050.455 (ebook) | DDC 372.47/6—dc23
LC record available at https://lccn.loc.gov/2020010031
LC ebook record available at https://lccn.loc.gov/2020010032

ISBN 978-0-8077-6412-1 (paper)
ISBN 978-0-8077-6413-8 (hardcover)
ISBN 978-0-8077-7868-5 (ebook)

Printed on acid-free paper
Manufactured in the United States of America

Contents

Foreword Tom Bean   ix

Introduction   1

1. **Digital Tools to Support Disciplinary Literacy in
    Diverse K-5 Classrooms: An Overview**   5

    What Is Disciplinary Literacy?   5

    Why Disciplinary Literacy in Grades K-5?   6

    How Is Disciplinary Literacy Different
    From Content-Area Literacy?   8

    A Brief Note on Text   9

    The Challenges of Disciplinary Literacy in Grades K-5   10

    The Goals of Disciplinary Literacy in Grades K-5   12

    How Can Digital Tools Support K-5 Disciplinary
    Literacy in Diverse K-5 Classrooms?   12

    What Does Current Research Suggest?   13

    Core Disciplinary Practices as an
    Approach to Disciplinary Literacy   14

2. **The PEDDL Framework**   19

    Planning for Disciplinary Literacy in Elementary Grades   20

    PEDDL Framework Overview   21

    Phase 1: Identifying Appropriate Disciplinary Literacy Practices   23

    Phase 2: Framing Disciplinary Literacy   25

    Phase 3: Selecting Multimodal Texts for Disciplinary Literacy   27

    Phase 4: Assessing Disciplinary Literacy with a Variety of Tools   30

    Phase 5: Digitally Supporting Disciplinary Literacy Instruction   32

Phase 6: Reflecting to Reach All Learners 35

Considerations for Diverse Learners in the PEDDL Framework 37

General Ideas for Practice 39

3. **Examining Disciplinary Literacy in
Elementary English Language Arts** 40

Integrating Disciplinary Literacy into ELA 40

How Can Disciplinary Literacy Instruction
Be Digitally Supported in ELA? 46

4. **Practical Approaches to Digitally Supported
Disciplinary Literacy in ELA** 52

Sample Lesson: Examining Culturally Diverse Fairytales
Through Literary Text Analysis in 2nd Grade 52

Questions to Ponder 63

5. **Examining Disciplinary Literacy in Elementary Mathematics** 64

Integrating Disciplinary Literacy into Mathematics 64

How Can Disciplinary Literacy Instruction
Be Digitally Supported in Mathematics? 71

6. **Practical Approaches to Digitally Supported
Disciplinary Literacy in Mathematics** 77

Sample Lesson:
Representing and Explaining Addition in Kindergarten 77

Questions to Ponder 85

7. **Examining Disciplinary Literacy in Elementary Science** 87

Integrating Disciplinary Literacy into Science 87

How Can Disciplinary Literacy Instruction
Be Digitally Supported in Science? 94

8. **Practical Approaches to Digitally Supported
Disciplinary Literacy in Science** 101

Sample Lesson: Evidence-Based Account
of Illumination in 1st Grade 101

Questions to Ponder 110

9. **Examining Disciplinary Literacy in Elementary Social Studies**   **111**

Integrating Disciplinary Literacy into Social Studies   111

How Can Disciplinary Literacy Instruction
Be Digitally Supported in Social Studies?   120

10. **Practical Approaches to Digitally Supported
Disciplinary Literacy in Social Studies**   **125**

Sample Lesson: Comprehending Multiple Types of Texts
to Better Understand U.S. Colonial Life in 5th grade   125

Questions to Ponder   134

11. **Closing Thoughts and Tips for Planning**   **136**

Long-Range Planning   136

Time, Time, Time   139

Designing Instruction That Is Appropriate for All Students   140

Introducing New Digital Tools to Students   140

Discrepancies Across Grades K–5   141

Explicit Disciplinary Literacy Instruction   142

Establishing a Professional Learning Network   143

Final Remarks   144

References   **145**

Index   **151**

About the Authors   **158**

Foreword

Does it seem strange to you that we assign phrases like "learning to read" to elementary students and "reading to learn" to middle and secondary students as if there is some magic zone where big disciplinary questions can be tackled? The authors of this compelling book move beyond those borders, providing K–5 teachers a roadmap for guiding students' exploration of disciplinary discourse and specific resources to tap into digital tools that make disciplinary learning exciting and engaging.

So, what are some big questions students can tackle rather than awaiting entry to the "reading to learn zone?" A few come to mind: global warming, plastics pollution in our waterways, sea level rise, disease pandemics, and the sheer weight of being a democratic citizen. Why wait to tackle these important issues? Rather, our K–5 classrooms can build a solid foundation of disciplinary exploration along with the application of digital tools.

Disciplinary literacy engages K–5 students in the unique nature and particularities of multiple subjects. These include elementary English language arts, mathematics, science, and social studies. This book features practical approaches to integrating these multiple subjects with digital tools to support students' learning.

Digitally Supported Disciplinary Literacy for Diverse K–5 Classrooms includes chapters that address three key areas: elementary reading acquisition, disciplinary vocabulary and comprehension, and the application of digital literacy tools for creative student engagement.

Rather than delaying introducing students to disciplinary literacy until middle and high school, the authors provide a framework for this process where readers can follow a 3rd-grade teacher, Ms. Branch, through vignettes that illustrate how she engages her students in active, problem-based learning. Each background chapter dives deeply into multiple examples, standards-based elements, and examples to illustrate the three focal areas of reading acquisition, disciplinary literacy, and digital applications. Indeed, this is a rich resource designed to transform elementary literacy teaching in powerful ways.

Each discipline encompasses both general and technical vocabulary that students are learning and that is a common element across disciplines. In addition, students working with informational texts and texts broadly defined to include digital representations like charts, graphs, and timelines need scaffolding in various disciplines. The affordances of digital applications to support students' creative ideas and share their findings with stakeholders (e.g., teachers, other classrooms, their peers) embrace a future where to be "literate" means being able to use multimodal representations.

The authors center this work on four key disciplinary elements:

- Recognizing and comprehending multiple text types
- Analyzing text
- Using vocabulary particular to a discipline
- Communicating an argument, rationalization, or understanding

These elements are fleshed out in detail across the 11 chapters and extensive examples in the online appendices. Various digital tools are illustrated with visual tables that provide a rich array of teaching resources.

Most importantly, the authors address the fact that moving into disciplinary literacy is a change process that can be adopted incrementally. Recognizing that changing one's approach to literacy teaching is never easy, a wealth of practical lesson examples helps readers move out of their comfort zones. In addition, each of the authors brings extensive classroom experience in classroom research, teacher professional development in disciplinary literacy, and leading-edge knowledge of digital tools.

The "Questions to Ponder" feature at the close of the practical approaches chapters helps dispel any anxiety over adopting a disciplinary literacy approach to elementary English language arts, mathematics, science, and social studies. In addition, the online appendices include sample lesson templates in each discipline.

In summary, if we want to enable future citizens to participate as "insiders" in a discipline, to critically analyze claims and assertions, and to represent and communicate information using digital tools, then the curriculum changes advocated in this book seem more important than ever.

—Thomas W. Bean, PhD,
Professor of Reading/Literacy,
Rosanne Keeley Norris Endowed Professor, Old Dominion University,
Darden College of Education and Professional Studies,
Department of Teaching and Learning
Norfolk, VA 23529

Introduction

We are not digital natives. We, the authors of this text, did not grow up using digital technology and we did not learn how to integrate technology into instruction in our teacher preparation programs. Rather, all of the authors of this book are former classroom teachers and current teacher educators who have come to value digital technology for the powerful ways that it can support the teaching and development of reading, writing, and communication skills in the academic disciplines, also referred to as *disciplinary literacy*. Namely, we have witnessed firsthand the more intricate and complex literacy skills required by revised state and national standards in the disciplines of English language arts, mathematics, science, and social studies. For example, elementary students may be asked to read across sources in history, engage in scientific inquiry, consider perspective in English, and seek solutions to real-world problems in mathematics. For many students, these skills require new ways of approaching the reading and writing of texts, and of thinking about what a text is in different disciplines, which may pose challenges when supporting a range of academically, culturally, linguistically, and socioeconomically diverse students.

However, our teacher training programs took a broad look at literacy, without much attention to literacy skills particular to disciplines of study. Yet, like you, we had to quickly learn and adapt to new technologies and standards as best we could, often with those technologies and standards being moving targets each year. It never became easier, per se, but we learned techniques to take what we were already doing and planning for, and revise those methods to integrate new approaches and digital tools.

Indeed, as teacher educators and researchers who spend a significant amount of time in K–12 classrooms, we see many needs, challenges, and possibilities that we hope to address in this book. First, we see the powerful potential of incorporating disciplinary literacy into diverse K–5 classrooms. Simultaneously, we see the difficulty of bringing disciplinary literacy practices into diverse classrooms of learners who are still developing basic reading and writing skills.

We also see the power of helping students in the elementary grades develop foundational understandings of the distinct reading, writing, and communication skills particular to each discipline of study (math, science, social studies) rather than waiting until they reach middle school and suddenly are expected to read complex disciplinary texts and communicate their understandings in sophisticated ways.

Yet, we also see, and have experienced, obstacles in implementing this type of instruction in the elementary grades. It is through these obstacles that we consider the powerful potential of using digital tools to support students with a variety of needs, experiences, and competencies in learning the distinct reading, writing, and communication skills particular to each discipline of study. Additionally, we see the power of students using digital tools to demonstrate their understanding and communicate about their learning. However, we also understand the challenges of effectively integrating digital tools into instruction, and the knowledge, experience, and understanding such integration may require. Put simply, we know that both disciplinary literacy and using digital tools in instruction are complex teaching practices, but we believe the value of both outweighs the challenges we, as well as teachers with whom we have worked, encounter.

We approached the writing of this book with the understanding that, from a discipline-specific perspective, elementary teachers often are trained in content-area literacy, which focuses on general strategy instruction to support literacy skills across content areas, instead of disciplinary literacy that has a singular focus on practices, or approaches of study, particular to a discipline. While we highly value content-area literacy and the strategies it offers, and will discuss it in greater detail in subsequent chapters as a supporting component of disciplinary literacy, we recognize that the more recent focus of learning in the elementary disciplines leans more heavily toward regarding each discipline as unique and teaching students to read, write, and communicate in ways that are specific to the discipline at hand. Therefore, we work to make connections when possible between the two areas of literacy, particularly as we focus on elementary students who still need ample literacy support in learning in the content areas.

As teacher educators, we have spent substantial time developing and studying methods for helping teachers effectively integrate digital technology into their instruction and for helping teachers incorporate disciplinary literacy practices in their diverse K–5 classrooms. In this book we bring together these ideas and approaches to help teachers design and plan for instruction in which students use digital tools to learn disciplinary literacy practices and communicate in disciplinary ways.

We open this book in Chapter 1 with research-based considerations and arguments for what we term *digitally supported disciplinary literacy* and how it might support diverse classrooms of students and student abilities. We define the particularities of disciplinary literacy instruction in grades K–5 and how digital tools might support such instruction. To guide teachers in designing this type of instruction, we developed the Planning Elementary Digitally Supported Disciplinary Literacy (PEDDL) Framework, which we present in Chapter 2 of this book. Chapter 2 also offers a PEDDL Planning Template—readily usable to begin planning digitally supported disciplinary literacy instruction. Additionally, beginning in Chapter 2, we introduce Ms. Branch, a 3rd-grade teacher at Wildwood Elementary School with 12 years of experience teaching grades K–5. Both Ms. Branch and her school are fictional, but they are representative of elementary teachers and schools that we have worked with. We follow Ms. Branch throughout this book to illustrate the techniques, practices, and skills that are essential to digitally supported disciplinary literacy.

In Chapters 3–10 we use a paired-chapter approach to delve deeply into each of the four disciplines of focus (English language arts: Chapters 3–4, math: Chapters 5–6, science: Chapters 7–8, and social studies: Chapters 9–10). We provide considerations and background related to planning digitally supported disciplinary literacy instruction, and then detailed lesson plan examples to illustrate these considerations. Throughout these chapters we also present an array of digital tools and practices, such as coding tools for creating stories and demonstrating learning, virtual reality (VR) tools for creating representations of ideas, and digital authoring tools for creating multimodal responses as a form of assessment. At the end of each "Practical Approaches" chapter (Chapters 4, 6, 8, and 10), you will find Questions to Ponder. These questions represent our recognition that planning and implementing digitally supported disciplinary literacy instruction in the elementary grades is not an easy task. Teachers are bound to encounter numerous obstacles and questions in doing so. Thus, we have drawn on our classroom experiences to present some of these potential challenges in this book and offer suggestions and solutions for navigating them. We also provide vignettes focusing on Ms. Branch and how she approaches integrating digitally supported disciplinary literacy into her classroom. We hope these vignettes serve as visualization for what teachers might encounter when considering this integration.

Throughout this book we draw on research, including our own, from the field of literacy to help teachers understand the need for disciplinary literacy instruction in the elementary grades, the ways that digital technology can support disciplinary learning, and how to use digital tools to support all learners in developing disciplinary literacy practices. We believe this research will provide useful evidence that the practices presented in this book, when planned and implemented thoughtfully, can work for students.

Ultimately, this book focuses on giving students the skills they need to ignite their curiosity and passion for learning and discovery, and preparing them for a knowledge-driven future. In turn, these exploration-focused skills may promote curiosity, inquisitiveness, and even a passion related to a discipline. As a result, students may develop important disciplinary practices that provide foundational skills they need in order to prepare for future careers in a given field.

CHAPTER 1

Digital Tools to Support Disciplinary Literacy in Diverse K-5 Classrooms: An Overview

We live in a constantly changing world and society that have a direct effect on how we teach our students. Learning standards, equitable learning environments, and digitally relevant instruction are three areas of education that have emerged as instructionally important during the 21st century, creating multiple considerations for teaching and planning instruction.

WHAT IS DISCIPLINARY LITERACY?

First, national and individual state standards require that students develop advanced literacy skills in earlier grades than ever before, involving different ways of thinking about how to develop appropriate and relevant literacy instruction at the K–5 levels. Thus, there has been a reconceptualization of literacy that has somewhat shifted what it means to be literate in each discipline of study (i.e., English, mathematics, science, and social studies), often referred to as *disciplinary literacy*. Further, the proliferation of digital tools and texts has shifted our understanding of what it means to be literate and what counts as text (Dalton, 2012). Disciplinary literacy has gained traction in K–12 learning because it promotes an investigative and real-world-focused approach to learning in the content areas. Instead of focusing on rote facts, disciplinary literacy often considers how students might use evidence and artifacts in each discipline to develop their own conclusions and relate their learning to real-life settings. This type of learning highlights critical thinking and a more democratic approach to learning. Likewise, support for the development of digital skills in literacy learning, alongside print-based literacy skills, has gained traction in K–12 learning because of the infinite possibilities technology offers for modifying, responding to, creating, and consuming text.

Second, literacy instruction that adequately prepares students for life and future learning must mirror the demands of the outside world. As technology continues to expand and integrate into many areas of daily life, digital tools hold much potential for keeping classroom instruction relevant. These tools also may support all students in literacy learning, placing a large focus on appropriate and supportive technology use in instruction. Through engagement in the use of digital tools for instructional purposes, students can be better prepared to consider the purpose and value of digital tools in their personal and post-school lives for information, communication, problem solving, and more.

Finally, classrooms are more diverse than ever before in regard to race, culture, socioeconomic status, and first languages. Although the focus of this book is on digital technologies and disciplinary literacy, we believe that instruction aimed to support all learners, and help learners connect personally to instruction, aligns with socially and culturally responsive teaching. Indeed, school enrollment statistics for Fall 2018 show that just over 26 million, or roughly half, of K–12 students in the United States are from historically minority races and cultures (National Center for Education Statistics, 2018b). These statistics predict that through at least 2027, the percentage of White and Black students will decline as the percentages of Hispanic and Asian students increase. Further, 19% of students live in poverty, with the majority being in a racial minority (National Center for Education Statistics, 2018b). Yet, recent teacher demographic surveys reveal that teachers are still predominantly (80%) White and middle class, with 89% of elementary teachers identifying as female (Taie & Goldring, 2017). As race, gender, socioeconomic status, and culture take a more central role and focus in society, it is important that teachers be prepared to foster student learning through instruction that reaches and supports all students and types of learners.

This book takes a focused look at these considerations to provide usable suggestions and methods for digitally supported disciplinary literacy instruction. To clarify, this book is not a manual on creating mini-disciplinarians. Instead, we hope to magnify the importance, usefulness, and applicability of Core Disciplinary Practices to develop more socially and academically adept students and to highlight how digital tools can support these relevant disciplinary literacy practices in young learners.

WHY DISCIPLINARY LITERACY IN GRADES K–5?

Disciplinary literacy has been and continues to be a topic of increasing importance in literacy education (Moje, 2008, 2015; Shanahan & Shanahan, 2012), and its principles have begun to extend into elementary grades (Brock, Goatley, Raphael, Trost-Shahata, & Weber, 2014; Shanahan & Shanahan, 2014) as a result of state and national standards (e.g., Common Core State Standards [CCSS]; National Governors Association Center for

Best Practices & Council of Chief State School Officers [NGACBP & CCSS], 2010). In light of this increasing importance, we, as teacher educators, are charged with helping elementary teachers promote disciplinary literacy. Put broadly, disciplinary literacy consists of the practices and skills required for someone to comprehend and actively participate in the study of a discipline, such as math, science, or history, in ways similar to how an expert, such as a mathematician, scientist, or historian, does (Moje, 2008; Shanahan & Shanahan, 2008, 2012). This perspective suggests that literacy transforms in meaning when considered in the context of the different disciplines of study, and that context is critical to determining what literacy skills students should learn.

Central to the idea of disciplinary literacy is that those in different academic disciplines, often referred to as *content areas*, read, write, and communicate differently. While on the surface this may seem like a forgone conclusion, it is a bit more complex than it seems. Disciplinary literacy refers to not only how particular disciplines engage in literacy practices, but also how those literacy practices inform understanding and thinking within the discipline itself (Shanahan & Shanahan, 2014). In short, disciplinary literacy raises the question, "What skills should students learn and be able to *use* to be able to read, write, and communicate in a specific discipline?" Arguably, these skills may better prepare students for participation in real-world contexts that require inquiry-focused practices (Moje, 2008, 2015).

We also believe that elementary students are capable of engaging in practices similar to mathematicians, scientists, historians, or literary scholars, albeit at a more basic level and with proper scaffolding (Juel, Hebard, Haubner, & Moran, 2010; VanSledright, 2002), that support explicit literacy instruction. And, current research suggests that this integration is possible and holds potential for engaging young students in inquiry learning (Britt & Ming, 2017; Maloch & Horsey, 2013; Wright & Gotwals, 2017). For example, from a disciplinary standpoint, digital and nondigital images, songs, maps, natural artifacts, photos, and audio recordings are all texts that can be read and comprehended, creating opportunities for even the youngest learners to engage in this type of study. Learning with these types of informational texts engages students in inquiry-based learning (Maloch & Horsey, 2013), which aligns with a disciplinary focus (Moje, 2015). Additionally, this learning exposes students to a variety of sources to consider in learning, which may promote a more culturally relevant approach as students learn from multiple viewpoints and construct knowledge based on a variety of perspectives that they may relate to real-world scenarios (Colwell, 2019; Peck, 2010; Toppel, 2015).

Disciplinary literacy differs from previously favored approaches to literacy in the content areas. Specifically, literacy in the content areas historically was focused on incorporating generalizable reading and writing strategies that could be used across disciplines to aid students in comprehending largely print-based text. While these types of strategies are certainly important and are useful in supporting reading and writing in the disciplines, we consider that disciplinary literacy skills are unique. Specifically, our students, even at early ages, are presented with problems outside of school that require them to use analytical thinking skills and engage with a number of text types, highlighting the importance of disciplinary literacy aims. Consider the following scenarios:

- A 5-year-old has to decide how many play objects can fit inside an overnight bag so that it closes properly and is still light enough for him to carry to a neighborhood friend's house for a first sleepover.
- A 9-year-old plants and cultivates a garden with her grandfather.
- An 8-year-old gets to vote on the service activity his Boy Scout troop will provide for the community.
- A 10-year-old who is interested in World War II reads *The War That Saved My Life* by Kimberly Brubaker Bradley over summer break.

Each of these scenarios requires different types of skills that also may be promoted through disciplinary study. These scenarios require application of learning in the disciplines to real-world events, emphasizing the usefulness of disciplinary literacy. Specifically, the 5-year-old uses mathematical skills to pack his bag. The 9-year-old engages in scientific practices related to earth sciences. Voting requires research and components of citizenship promoted in social studies. And, the 10-year-old must use disciplinary practices in English when reading and considering a historical fiction novel. Indeed, each discipline targets important skills that may be useful in supporting young learners in inquiry, analysis, and application of learning.

HOW IS DISCIPLINARY LITERACY
DIFFERENT FROM CONTENT-AREA LITERACY?

Literacy, especially in the present day, encompasses a myriad of skills ranging from basic decoding of text to the ability to understand and navigate text on the Internet. Varying viewpoints exist on the exact traits that being literate in the disciplines, or content areas, entails. Years ago, Moore, Readence, and Rickelman (1983) recognized that to be successful studying in the content areas, adolescent students need to develop and use more advanced strategies to read and comprehend higher level texts. Defining and developing those more advanced strategies have grounded content-area literacy across K–12 grades and has been at the forefront of literacy during the previous 4 decades. Many students struggle with comprehension when reading texts in content areas, and literacy strategies (e.g., KWL, Readers' Theater, Fishbowl Discussions,

RAFT Writing) that support content-area learning may be necessary for students to successfully navigate content-area texts.

However, literature has emerged more recently that indicates that such general literacy strategies, when used out of context of the goals of a discipline, may not be the best approach to helping students understand and analyze disciplinary texts. In other words, just being able to comprehend a text's message might not translate into critical or advanced thinking in a discipline. As a result, disciplinary literacy emerged as a new viewpoint from which to reconsider literacy in the content areas (Moje, 2008; Shanahan & Shanahan, 2008, 2012).

Whereas content-area literacy is focused on instruction in general strategies that can be used across disciplines to aid students in reading content-area texts, disciplinary literacy considers specific practices disciplinarians use to read and study texts in individual disciplines. We discuss these practices in more depth in Chapters 3, 5, 7, and 9. Disciplinary literacy, in that regard, is grounded in how experts approach and use texts in their respective disciplines (Juel et al., 2010; Moje, 2008; Shanahan & Shanahan, 2008; Wilson, 2011). Importantly, disciplinary literacy seeks to provide students with literacy-infused practices that promote disciplinary learning and with insight into why those practices are important and how they can be utilized in everyday life (Moje, 2008). Further, in conjunction with studying *how* to use disciplinary practices, disciplinary literacy includes the study of *why* these practices are important (Moje, 2008).

Disciplinary literacy emerged, in part, as a response to multiple barriers to integrating content-area reading strategies into content curricula (Draper & Siebert, 2010). Research indicated that general literacy strategies, when taught in isolation from content, do little to increase literacy skills (see Bean, 2000). Nevertheless, disciplinary literacy encourages the use of content literacy strategies to scaffold and support disciplinary learning, as long as those strategies align with the practices of a discipline (Moje, 2015). Research suggests that students who struggle with language and literacy would benefit from the use of content literacy strategies in disciplinary instruction (Faggella-Luby, Graner, Deshler, & Drew, 2012). Thus, content literacy still plays a role in disciplinary learning, but teachers must consider what strategies best support a disciplinary approach to instruction. The chapters that provide lesson plan examples (Chapters 4, 6, 8, and 10) illustrate how content-area literacy strategies can be used in disciplinary literacy instruction with digital tools.

A BRIEF NOTE ON TEXT

We wish to highlight here that in this book we consider texts using a broad lens that encompasses any material that can be read, consumed, or interpreted (Draper & Siebert, 2010). Disciplinarians "read" a number of texts to inform their work, and many times those texts do not contain prose-based words. These texts are relevant to disciplinary literacy in K–5 classrooms as teachers will need to select texts that reflect the types of texts studied within the disciplines (Colwell, 2019). Such texts, with the exception of study in English language arts (ELA), will be primarily informational, which aligns with calls to integrate more informational texts into elementary grades (Shanahan & Shanahan, 2014). Thus, our use of the word *text* in this book might encompass a myriad of resources that can be consumed or produced, which we also feel expands opportunities to reach all learners.

THE CHALLENGES OF DISCIPLINARY LITERACY IN GRADES K-5

Unlike upper grades where content and disciplinary learning are the focus of instruction, elementary grades require greater attention to learning to read, write, and communicate during the study of content. Therefore, disciplinary literacy must take on a varied meaning at this level (Brock et al., 2014; Shanahan & Shanahan, 2014). Here, disciplinary literacy might focus more on acclimating and scaffolding students to comprehend disciplinary texts, understanding the differences between disciplines, and more critically considering multiple types of texts (Shanahan & Shanahan, 2014). In short, although elementary students are certainly capable of engaging in disciplinary literacy, they need instruction that supports learning in the disciplines as well as explicit literacy instruction to bolster their developing traditional literacy skills (Juel et al., 2010; VanSledright, 2002). This scaffolding and explicit instruction can better prepare students to engage in the types of literacy they will encounter in upper grades.

Another challenge to disciplinary literacy instruction is that literacy is linked almost solely with English language arts in elementary grades, where the majority of reading, writing, and communication skills are specifically taught. As such, common instructional approaches to literacy in K–5 highlight ELA integration and connections to mathematics, science, and social studies without any focus on the goals of those disciplines. For example, it is common to see historical fiction integrated into social studies to connect ELA and history. However, historians typically study primary sources and documents, and informational texts would be a more pertinent choice when promoting disciplinary literacy. While we recognize that these cross-content connections may be beneficial, they somewhat negate the deliberate teaching of disciplinary skills as literacy opportunities. Also, and importantly, this link reduces ELA instruction to the teaching of reading, writing, and communication, and lessens the focus on literature and literary composition, which is an integral practice of the ELA discipline. We, along with other researchers, view ELA, including literary analysis and composition, as its own distinct discipline (Håland, 2017; Shanahan & Shanahan, 2014; Smagorinsky, 2015; Spires, Kerkhoff, & Graham, 2016).

Further, today's K–5 classrooms are diverse in learning and language abilities, creating an array of skill levels, viewpoints, and perspectives in any one classroom. Unlike in middle and high school content classrooms, which often are sorted into general and advanced levels of study, elementary teachers must reach a variety of learners and ability levels in one class. Coupled with differences in students' backgrounds and languages, at first glance K–5 classrooms may seem to be particularly challenging settings for integrating disciplinary literacy. For example, disciplinary literacy promotes advanced skills of thinking, reasoning, and inquiry, which may be problematic for students who speak English as a second language or who struggle with traditional literacy skills.

However, multiple opportunities for and benefits of disciplinary literacy instruction exist in these grades. First, disciplinary literacy employs a wide variety of texts, which increases opportunities for students to come into contact with perspectives and cultural viewpoints similar to their own, as well as various text types. Also, disciplinary literacy focuses on addressing real-world issues, which may be more relevant and engaging for all students as they connect school to life. Finally, disciplinary literacy opens the door for studying multiple types of resources that go beyond the use of solely print-based texts. Indeed, a variety of tools and texts, both print and digital, are important to supporting disciplinary learning in elementary grades. Digital texts enable teachers to bring artifacts and experiences into the classroom that would not be accessible otherwise. For example, numerous Smithsonian exhibits and galleries can be viewed in 3-D, with detailed views through virtual reality experiences made available online. Similarly, digital tools enable students to create forms of response that otherwise would not be possible (Hutchison, Beschorner, & Schmidt-Crawford, 2012), accommodating a wider variety of students and student learning abilities. Consequently, it is important for elementary teachers to consider the role of digital texts and tools, and how to support students in using them, when planning disciplinary literacy instruction.

In brief, we are well aware of the challenges of disciplinary literacy in K–5 classrooms, yet the potential of disciplinary literacy outweighs these challenges. Our backgrounds in helping teachers use digital tools to support literacy and disciplinary learning (see Colwell & Hutchison, 2015; Hutchison, 2018; Hutchison & Beschorner, 2014; Hutchison et al., 2012; Hutchison & Colwell, 2014, 2016; Hutchison, Nadolny, & Estapa, 2016; Hutchison & Woodward, 2014a, 2014b, 2018; Thoma, Hutchison, Johnson, Johnson, & Stromer, 2017) provide a path to leveraging these challenges and potentialities and open the door to innovative approaches to elementary literacy instruction relevant to real-world scenarios and human populations.

THE GOALS OF DISCIPLINARY LITERACY IN GRADES K-5

Because K–5 instruction places a larger emphasis on learning to read and write and supporting those literacy skills, we note that the goals of disciplinary literacy in K–5 may vary somewhat from middle and secondary goals, where content typically takes center stage. Keeping both the challenges and the potentialities of disciplinary literacy in K–5 in mind, we created a list of instructional goals that teachers might reference in planning disciplinary literacy. Specifically, students will be:

1. exposed to texts, practices, and procedures that experts might use to study in a discipline.
2. given supervised and scaffolded practice using expert practices applicable to K–5 learning.
3. exposed to a variety of diverse texts and text types, in format, content, and authorship.
4. engaged in inquiry-focused learning and thinking that also build literacy skills.
5. provided with practice in reading and drawing conclusions based on multiple types of texts.
6. provided with expanded writing opportunities to incorporate various modes of creation and composition.
7. given multiple opportunities for student-centered learning that allow students to consider their diverse backgrounds and the positive attributes of those backgrounds.

HOW CAN DIGITAL TOOLS SUPPORT K-5 DISCIPLINARY LITERACY IN DIVERSE K-5 CLASSROOMS?

As noted, although elementary students are certainly capable of analysis, reasoning, and inquiry, grades K–5 pose a distinct challenge for disciplinary literacy instruction. It is in these grades that students are building and refining their reading, writing, and communication skills. Some students may still be learning to read in early elementary grades, or they may struggle to comprehend texts they read, due to a variety of reasons, including ability level, familiarity with text type or vocabulary, or native language. In elementary grades, we see the particular usefulness of digital tools to support disciplinary literacy, and we use the subsequent chapters in this book to provide recommendations for digitally supported disciplinary literacy.

First, however, we want to distinguish between an emerging concept termed *digital literacies for disciplinary learning* and our focus on digitally supported disciplinary literacy. Recently, digital literacies for disciplinary learning has been suggested as a framework and addressed as an important area in adolescent literacy (Castek & Manderino, 2017; Manderino & Castek, 2016). This area suggests that disciplinary literacy is critical to supporting and fostering digital literacy skills (e.g., online networking, accessing and synthesizing online information, and communicating information via web-based platforms), and vice versa. This means that these areas are "inextricably linked rather than separate areas of focus" (Manderino & Castek, 2016, p. 80). We agree that at the adolescent level of education, where digital tools and Internet exploration are more integral and used more seamlessly in and out of school, this concept certainly holds much promise and is relevant to literacy learning. However, at the elementary level, particularly in lower grades, students are still developing digital skills and are less able to explore the Internet at a more advanced level. We see digital tools as having a supporting, not equal, role in disciplinary literacy instruction.

From this perspective, we use the term *digitally supported disciplinary literacy* to indicate that teachers must first decide what disciplinary literacy skills they aim to teach, and then select digital tools that might support students in learning those skills. This is not to say that digital and disciplinary literacy are not connected in K–5 grades; instead, our focus is more on the appropriate selection of digital tools to support disciplinary literacy rather than linking digital and disciplinary literacy skills to each other. Indeed, as our earlier work has indicated (see Hutchison & Colwell, 2015), digital tools hold much potential for supporting literacy learning in elementary grades. We expand on this work to offer practical ideas, tools, and methods for teachers to use to support disciplinary literacy.

For example, students may be provided digital texts with audio technology to support burgeoning literacy skills. Digital tools also may help students organize their analytical thinking through annotation and graphic representation of ideas. Further, students may use digital tools to present their ideas in more detailed and complex formats that surpass their writing and communication abilities, and provide teachers with a more comprehensive understanding of students' disciplinary literacy skills. Certainly, as knowledge about disciplinary literacy instruction in elementary contexts continues to develop, so too does our understanding of how digital tools can support the development of students' disciplinary literacy skills alongside their reading skills. This remains a promising, but relatively new, area of K–5 education.

WHAT DOES CURRENT RESEARCH SUGGEST?

Although this book focuses on practical applications and uses of digital tools to support disciplinary literacy, we looked to research to support this application. For example, Liebfreund and Conradi (2016) called attention to the increasing use of informational texts in all elementary content areas, which encourages different approaches to text comprehension than those used with literary texts. Elementary teachers consistently use nontraditional texts, such as pictures, songs, art, and digital media, when working with young readers and writers, and focus on disciplinary methods for reading such texts. This expanded repertoire of texts, including digital texts that are common in elementary classrooms, supports integrating disciplinary literacy into earlier grades (Frambaugh-Kritzer, Buelow, & Steele, 2015; Shanahan & Shanahan, 2014).

Recently, Siffrinn and Lew (2018) addressed the important aspect of promoting disciplinary language to support elementary students. Academic language instruction has the potential to ensure more equitable access to disciplinary practices, as it fosters common understandings of disciplinary vocabulary and language structure without relying primarily on students' prior knowledge or experiences. Topics for language-specific instruction in their study involved the vocabulary and descriptive language used when measuring (mathematics) and recognizing and building simple machines (science). While the activities described were using traditional group or materials-based instruction, these two topics would have benefited from the consideration of digital tools to show different types and methods of measuring and additional ways to create and view simple machines, both of which would extend beyond the classroom. This not only would engage students in a space where they could bring their background knowledge and skills to show language use in a different way, but also would contribute to knowledge of the disciplinary practices in mathematics and science.

Similarly, Parenti (2018) offered a model of guided retelling to support disciplinary knowledge of recognizing patterns of text and disciplinary language patterns. Central to the concept of this approach to guided retelling are multimedia visual cues, with such examples as a "photo, pie graph, scatterplot, flyer, cartoon, flow chart, video, pamphlet" (p. 476), among others. We believe it is important to recognize the role that digital tools might play in teaching that draws on this instructional approach. Many of these visual cues are much more easily created using a digital tool, some require the use of a digital tool, and all would benefit from discipline-specific instruction focused on visual representations of information.

This research recognizes the role that digital tools play in elementary disciplinary literacy instruction, and how intentional planning to support students in engaging with those digital tools can develop students' literacy and disciplinary knowledge.

CORE DISCIPLINARY PRACTICES
AS AN APPROACH TO DISCIPLINARY LITERACY

As a starting point for disciplinary literacy instruction, we must think about what skills disciplinary experts use when they study or work within their discipline so that we can reimagine what literacy might look like from this perspective. This perspective is important, as experts engage in disciplinary study because they seek to answer socially relevant questions (Moje, 2015). Educators then must consider how disciplinary skills translate to school settings (Draper, Broomhead, Jensen, & Siebert, 2010). Particularly, as we focus on grades K–5, we must consider what disciplinary skills are both *important* and *appropriate* for building literacy within the disciplines, and how those skills might best be supported in these early grades.

Table 1.1 provides a brief overview of the practices that experts use to study in the core disciplines. Note that this table is not comprehensive or exhaustive, as we discuss each discipline in more detail in subsequent chapters. Additionally, while we acknowledge that there are multiple disciplines that converge to form the elementary curriculum, we focus on the four core disciplinary areas in which general education elementary teachers typically provide instruction.

Notably, each core discipline focuses on specific practices of study. We know that, for K–5 teachers who are charged with teaching multiple disciplines often in the same day, these practices may seem overwhelming. However, our aim with this book is to make disciplinary literacy instruction feasible. In doing so, we want to provide a way to think about disciplinary literacy in your own classroom, how digital tools might support disciplinary literacy, and how you might reach all of your students through this type of instruction. To this end, we recognize that K–5 disciplinary literacy instruction may need to be approached a bit differently than in the upper grades. The primary areas of focus should be to provide students with a solid foundation of skills relevant to disciplinary literacy, to provide experiences with different types of informational texts, and to give opportunities to discern approaches of study in each discipline (Shanahan & Shanahan, 2014). Thus, we read across practices in the disciplines to provide teachers with what we have termed *Core Disciplinary Practices*, as follows, that might be used, with some modification, in each of the K–5 disciplines:

1. Recognizing and comprehending multiple text types
2. Analyzing text
3. Using vocabulary particular to a discipline
4. Communicating an argument, rationalization, or understanding

These four practices are integrated throughout the remainder of this book and are introduced here to provide a foundation for later discipline-specific discussion.

Table 1.1. Disciplinary Practices Overview

Discipline	Disciplinary Practices
English Language Arts	• Exploring textual patterns • Examining strange aspects of text • Reading across multiple types of texts to gain understandings of the human experience • Making original text-based claims • Communicating to a variety of audiences • Posing a problem or question and reading across texts to develop a conclusion (International Literacy Association & National Council of Teachers of English, 1996/2012; Rainey, 2016)
Mathematics	• Building, adapting, and applying knowledge through problem solving • Using reasoning and proof • Evaluating mathematical arguments • Communicating mathematical thinking • Relating mathematical ideas to one another and in contexts outside of mathematics • Creating representations to communicate mathematical understandings • Creating/understanding algorithms (National Council of Teachers of Mathematics [NCTM], 2000, 2013)
Science	• Asking questions and defining problems • Using and developing models • Conducting investigations • Using mathematical and computational thinking • Building explanations • Evaluating reports • Communicating findings (Next Generation Science Standards Lead States, 2013)
Social Studies	**History** • Analyzing past evidence to understand events and timelines • Sourcing primary texts and information • Contextualizing primary sources **Civics** • Rationalizing and reasoning the law and rules of society **Economics** • Analyzing production and consumption of goods based on supply and demand • Forecasting or theorizing economic outlook based on multiple data **Geography** • Analyzing physical and human characteristics of a region to inform history, politics, and natural phenomena (National Council for the Social Studies [NCSS], 2013)

Recognizing and Comprehending Multiple Text Types

This Core Disciplinary Practice emphasizes the need for teachers to design instruction that supports the development of reading comprehension skills in the disciplines, while also acknowledging that students encounter a variety of text types that may require unique comprehension skills and strategies. For example, the strategies that may best support students' comprehension of a news article may differ from the strategies that might support their comprehension of a photograph from that news article. Additionally, while reading the text in the digital news story on a news site, students may need to employ strategies for making inferences about the text to determine when it may be useful to click a hyperlink. The same strategy would not be useful in the same way in a print-based news story since that text would not contain hyperlinks. Further, particularly in earlier elementary grades, recognition of the types of texts that are specific to each discipline is an important foundational skill for students to acquire. One way that young students who are still developing traditional reading skills might engage in disciplinary literacy is to begin to sort and recognize the types of texts that are found in each of the disciplines.

Analyzing Text

Text analysis and critique is an essential practice for being a skilled reader in any discipline. It can be especially difficult for elementary students to analyze, critique, and comprehend expository texts used in subjects like science and social studies because these texts often deal with unfamiliar ideas (Duke, 2010); students are not exposed to expository texts as often as fictional texts (Duke, 2000); and expository texts are often poorly organized (Beck, McKeown, Sinatra, & Loxterman, 1991). Even so, scholars have demonstrated that teaching elementary students to analyze text structure in content-area texts leads to improved comprehension (Marinak & Gambrell, 2008).

In addition to analyzing text structures, students should be guided to consider issues of power, perspective, and social equity when reading any text (Luke & Freebody, 1999). Text structures and the issues and perspectives that must be considered vary substantially by text type. For example, the way that one must consider the perspectives represented in a science textbook is different from the way one must consider the perspectives represented in a video. Similarly, the structure of a science textbook and the structure of a video on a science topic create different demands for readers, yet both are common texts in elementary grades. Thus, analyzing and critiquing texts is a Core Disciplinary Practice for disciplinary reading and writing.

Using Vocabulary Particular to a Discipline

The Core Disciplinary Practice of teaching students to comprehend and use vocabulary particular to a discipline addresses several concerns related to disciplinary literacy. A strong indicator of disciplinary literacy is fluency in the language and thinking habits of a discipline. Understanding the academic vocabulary and being able to use the language of a discipline are essential parts of being literate in a discipline. Yet, each discipline has unique academic language, and vocabulary instruction should not be the same across content areas (Shanahan & Shanahan, 2012). According to those authors, teaching students a uniform set of strategies for understanding vocabulary terms across content areas does not adequately support students because it does not attend to discipline-specific distinctions. Further, early exposure to ideas and common features of academic vocabulary is important in laying a foundation for later vocabulary learning in school. Thus, teachers must carefully consider appropriate strategies for supporting comprehension and use of academic language in each discipline, with an emphasis on understanding why vocabulary terms are constructed in the way they are in each discipline.

Communicating an Argument, Rationalization, or Understanding

While the first three Core Disciplinary Practices focus on consumption and consideration of texts, this fourth practice focuses on the production of text to present disciplinary understanding. This Core Disciplinary Practice provides an important platform for students to illustrate their disciplinary learning and comprehension in the disciplines. As we think about elementary learning and instruction, we also must think about assessment and how disciplinary literacy will be evaluated. Providing a space for students to write, construct, or compose an argument, rationalization, or understanding in the disciplines using multiple platforms allows them to use traditional and digitally focused literacy skills to showcase their disciplinary literacy learning. In turn, this practice provides a bridge for traditional and disciplinary literacy in a dually beneficial manner. This practice also allows for multiple evidence-based interpretations of texts studied in the disciplines, allowing all learners to display their individual learning, using platforms that are most appropriate for their background and learning abilities.

CHAPTER 2

The PEDDL Framework

Wildwood Elementary School serves grades K–5 and enrolls a diverse population of students. Wildwood Elementary has a 76% free and reduced lunch rate; 22% of students are English language learners; 20% are African American, 9% Asian, 26% Hispanic, 6% multiracial, 1% Native American or Pacific Islander, and 38% White; and 15% of students are in special education programs. Ms. Branch, a 3rd-grade teacher, has 26 students in her class, about half of whom were reading on grade level when they entered 2nd grade. Her students reflect the diversity in the school, and she has six students who are English language learners. This year, Ms. Branch is seeking to reframe some of her literacy instruction around mathematics, social studies, and science, based on her state's newly revised standards that highlight discipline-specific thinking skills.

Previously, when focusing on literacy in these subjects, Ms. Branch made connections to English language arts and used children's literature that seemed to relate to applicable topics in these subject areas. Ms. Branch found this approach appealing because it helped her to make connections to students' backgrounds, which she finds critical in planning instruction. Yet, although students' ELA skills were supported in this instruction, Ms. Branch noticed that skills directly related to studying math, science, and social studies, which are targeted in the revised standards, became of secondary importance.

Additionally, a recent initiative at Ms. Branch's school has promoted literacy as a way to extend students' conception of reading, writing, and communication beyond the instruction they receive in the classroom and in connection to the outside world, particularly related to digital tools. For example, Wildwood highlighted a literacy "star" each week, and staff modeled for students various literacy practices they engaged in outside of school, such as the principal who changed his eating habits after following nutrition blogs, the bus driver who shares short poems on his YouTube channel, the librarian who is tracing her family ancestry via Internet resources, and a 5th-grade teacher who designs toy trucks using a 3-D printer. Ms. Branch believes that understanding how literacy practices, such as reading, writing, composition, and communication, look in the outside world may help her students better understand the importance of in-school literacy learning. She also likes that these practices can connect students' interests and backgrounds to their learning. Further, Ms. Branch has a keen interest in using digital tools because she knows that they can support learners who sometimes struggle with reading and writing. She decides that it will be beneficial for her students if she redesigns or updates her instruction to reflect recent changes in her state's standards and her school, but she is somewhat unsure of where to begin.

PLANNING FOR DISCIPLINARY LITERACY IN ELEMENTARY GRADES

One reason, perhaps the main reason, for writing this book is to respond to the challenges of planning for elementary disciplinary literacy. In particular, elementary teachers face the unique task of considering literacy in multiple disciplines (e.g., English language arts, history, geography, science, mathematics) on a daily basis. Additionally, elementary instruction often is planned, guided, and paced through particular textbooks, readers, and resources selected by state or local school districts and divisions. Completely revising content instruction is out of the question, nor do we wish to ask teachers to use even more of their valuable planning time to redevelop instruction that they already have spent considerable time planning.

Thus, while resources exist that address disciplinary literacy in the elementary grades (e.g., Altieri, 2011; Brock et al., 2014), we sought to develop a usable comprehensive framework for helping teachers to think through various aspects of their current instruction and consider how they might extend that instruction to support disciplinary literacy practices.

Although disciplinary literacy, as a perspective, indicates that each discipline is unique, as are the practices specific to each discipline, we argue that elementary grades differ from upper grades in how content instruction is approached. Thus, planning for disciplinary literacy in elementary grades will not look the same or require the same approaches as it would in upper grades (Shanahan & Shanahan, 2014). Therefore, we focus on the Core Disciplinary Practices we defined in Chapter 1 that may be used in each discipline, albeit in different ways that highlight the uniqueness of each core discipline. We provide these practices again here for reference:

1. Recognizing and comprehending multiple text types
2. Analyzing text
3. Using vocabulary particular to a discipline
4. Communicating an argument, rationalization, or understanding

We have found in our work with teachers that providing such practices as a starting point to think about disciplinary literacy integration is beneficial. As teachers become more familiar with integrating these Core Disciplinary Practices into their instruction, they often begin to target additional self-selected disciplinary practices. Thus, these Core Disciplinary Practices are just a starting point. We believe that limiting focus to these four practices will expose elementary students to the concept of disciplinary literacy and allow early interaction with higher-level reading, writing, and thinking skills to build a foundation for using more advanced disciplinary practices in future upper grades.

PEDDL FRAMEWORK OVERVIEW

The Planning Elementary Digitally Supported Disciplinary Literacy Framework is designed to support elementary teachers in integrating disciplinary literacy Core Disciplinary Practices into their instruction, which according to state and national standards is a necessity for most teachers across the United States. As can be seen in Table 2.1, this framework is designed in consideration of the planning that teachers already do to prepare for content instruction in their classroom and offers guiding questions to prompt disciplinary literacy extensions of existing instruction.

Table 2.1. Planning Elementary Digitally Supported Disciplinary Literacy Framework

Current Instructional Considerations	Disciplinary Extensions
PHASE 1: Identifying Appropriate Disciplinary Literacy Practices	
• What state/national standards am I targeting? • What are my lesson objectives?	• What Core Disciplinary Practices are supported by those standards and objectives?
PHASE 2: Framing Disciplinary Literacy	
• What information is important for my students to learn and understand from this lesson?	• Why is it important for students to learn and understand this topic? • What essential question(s) might frame the importance of understanding this topic?
PHASE 3: Selecting Multimodal Texts for Disciplinary Literacy	
• What texts does my school or school district require when teaching this topic? • What texts do I feel comfortable using to support students' learning? • Which topical texts align with my students' current reading levels?	• What digital and multimodal texts might supplement my currently used texts and extend students' learning to encourage disciplinary literacy? • How might these digital and multimodal texts help support students to engage in more advanced reading, writing, and communication practices?

(table continues on next page)

Table 2.1. Planning Elementary Digitally Supported Disciplinary Literacy Framework *(continued)*

Current Instructional Considerations	Disciplinary Extensions
PHASE 4: Assessing Disciplinary Literacy with a Variety of Tools	
• What assessments do I currently use to determine students' learning and understanding of this topic? • What type(s) of knowledge (e.g., fact-based, process-based, etc.) do those assessments gauge?	• How can I incorporate digital tools to further assess students' understanding of disciplinary practices and texts? • How do these digital tools create or support a more comprehensive assessment of students' understanding?
PHASE 5: Digitally Supporting Disciplinary Literacy Instruction	
• How do I prepare my students to learn this topic?	• What digital tools extend and deepen students' preparation to learn this topic?
• How do I guide my students' comprehension of this topic?	• What digital tools can I incorporate to scaffold students' disciplinary comprehension and analysis of multiple types of texts?
• How do I help my students reflect on their learning of this topic?	• What digital tools support and extend students' synthesis of learning of this topic? • What digital tools support students' development of artifacts to illustrate disciplinary literacy?
PHASE 6: Reflecting to Reach All Learners	
• How have I differentiated instruction in this lesson?	• How have I considered personal, social, and cultural understandings that inform this lesson? • Are the texts I have selected responsive to students' personal, social, and/or cultural backgrounds? • Have I provided multiple types of assessments, and at least one authentic assessment, to accurately determine all students' progress and understanding of the topic? • How have I differentiated instruction in this lesson to reach a variety of cultural, socioeconomic, and linguistic backgrounds?

While we hope that teachers find opportunities to revise whole lessons to support disciplinary literacy, we created the PEDDL Framework to also support small steps in disciplinary literacy instruction.

For instance, the framework is intended to support planning through the six phases, but teachers may choose to focus on a few phases at a time. Further, the framework builds on existing curriculum and instruction to aid in integration into current content and not addition of new content. Essentially, the PEDDL Framework promotes close attention to disciplinary literacy and how teachers might encourage this type of literacy in various aspects of their instruction. Particularly, this framework draws on integration of digital tools to expand all elementary students' learning and engagement in disciplinary practices, which we discuss throughout the remaining chapters, with supporting lesson plan examples. We highlight digital tools and consider them critical for elementary disciplinary literacy because, often, students can comprehend and organize more-complex disciplinary information at a more advanced level when they read and view digital texts than when they read traditional texts.

We note first that Phases 1 and 2 are the only phases in the framework that do not specifically focus on digital tools or texts. This is intentional in design. Although the focus of this book and the PEDDL Framework is on digitally supported disciplinary literacy for all learners, we believe, and research indicates, that digital tools should not be the primary consideration in instructional planning (Hutchison & Reinking, 2011; Hutchison & Woodward, 2014b). Instead, we use Phases 1 and 2 to help teachers identify disciplinary literacy practices and how to frame instruction of those practices so that they then may make informed decisions about the types of digital texts and tools that can support disciplinary learning. In the upcoming sections we provide detailed explanations of each phase of the PEDDL Framework and practical examples of how the phases support the design of digitally supported disciplinary literacy instruction.

PHASE 1:
IDENTIFYING APPROPRIATE DISCIPLINARY LITERACY PRACTICES

As with most instructional planning, planning for disciplinary literacy instruction involves identifying specific standards and lesson objectives and extending those standards and objectives into disciplinary literacy practices. A probable challenge when planning for disciplinary literacy in elementary school is the expectation that a teacher should be able to identify, understand, and engage students in the practices of multiple disciplines of study. Even in middle and secondary teacher education, where content is a large component of teacher preparation, these practices are not always made explicit in teacher preparation, and teachers may feel uncomfortable designing disciplinary literacy instruction (Shanahan & Shanahan, 2008). At the elementary level, where teachers are trained in multiple content areas, and traditional reading and writing are still at the forefront of instruction, this discomfort may be increased (Shanahan & Shanahan, 2014). For many elementary teachers, planning for disciplinary literacy is complex in that that they are uncertain of where to begin (Lemley, Hart, & King, 2019) and how to target disciplinary literacy (Siffrinn & Lew, 2018).

In this first phase, we tackle how to consider targeted instructional standards and connect those standards to a Core Disciplinary Practice in a selected discipline. We propose in this first phase of planning that learning standards serve as a starting point, as they normally do in daily and long-range planning, to identify Core Disciplinary Practices that may engage students in disciplinary literacy.

Phase 1 in Practice

Consider the following elementary social studies standard often targeted in 3rd or 4th grade:

The student will demonstrate skills for historical analysis, including the ability to draw conclusions and make generalizations.

This elementary standard directly outlines skills for "draw[ing] conclusions and mak[ing] generalizations" in historical analysis. The lesson objective for this standard might be: Compare and contrast accounts of Captain John Smith and Pocahontas to create a conclusion about their relationship and impact. Here, the act of analyzing text to draw conclusions from reading historical sources is a Core Disciplinary Practice that can be integrated into existing instruction. Notice how traditional literacy skills (text comprehension) play a large role in the greater disciplinary literacy skill of analysis of a historical text or texts. Disciplinary literacy often aligns with traditional literacy skills that are already a target of instruction, particularly in the elementary grades where reading and writing are highlighted across content areas. Yet, as we discussed in Chapter 1, disciplinary literacy focuses those literacy skills on a very specific component of the discipline (i.e., analysis and generalizations) that students need in order to be literate in history (Nokes, 2010; Wineburg, 1991). This first phase is intended to help elementary teachers consider how they might target Core Disciplinary Practices that can both support disciplinary literacy and continue to engage students in required literacy and content learning.

PHASE 2: FRAMING DISCIPLINARY LITERACY

Disciplinary literacy, at its core, supports an approach to learning that connects content to real-world relevance through a focus on how experts study in a discipline (Moje, 2015). Although in today's educational world, testing and standards are often primary considerations in planning instruction, disciplinary literacy encourages a broader purpose of instruction to create more informed and more engaged citizens who are prepared to effectively navigate the world. Thus, to promote disciplinary literacy, teachers may extend the overarching goal of instruction to align with this school-to-world connection. Phase 2 focuses on this extension, through the use of essential questions (EQs).

Teachers often pose questions to their students to promote content learning. For example, one question teachers may ask in a U.S. history lesson is: "Who was Pocahontas?" However, planning for disciplinary literacy suggests that teachers consider an overarching question to highlight the importance of studying a particular topic. "Who was Pocahontas" may elicit multiple responses, but it does not necessarily require students to critically analyze one or more sources of information to draw a conclusion. This question could be answered by reading a single biographical summary in a textbook. It is not our intent to undermine textbook information. Certainly, textbooks play a large role in elementary-grade learning, and the information gleaned from textbook reading is important and valuable in an elementary context where students are learning to comprehend informational sources and grounding foundational knowledge of historical figures. Yet, teachers may supplement the textbook with primary historical sources, which aligns more closely with how a historian studies history, and develop an overarching question to frame their lesson from a disciplinary literacy perspective. These overarching questions often are referred to as essential questions (Wiggins & McTighe, 2005).

Essential Questions

What is an essential question? Broadly speaking, essential questions are questions that frame a lesson and guide learning and discovery about content; they are typically unanswerable with a single response (Wiggins & McTighe, 2005). EQs often prompt further questions, driving investigation and analysis. Particularly, these questions frame standards-based learning to "focus on the big ideas that connect and bring meaning to all the discrete facts and skills" (Wiggins & McTighe, 2005, p. 105).

EQs stand in contrast to closed questions, which typically elicit a single correct answer. We argue that EQs need not take on any specific semantic format, but that the practices and activities that support EQs should be investigative and/or experimental in design. For example, although closed questions often have yes/no responses or simple fact responses, some of these types of questions may engage students in inquiry if the lesson allows students to participate in experiment or debate following their yes/no response (Wiggins & McTighe, 2005). Such activities will be supported by a variety of texts that students read, examine, and analyze, using procedures and activities appropriate to their learning and literacy levels. We provide Table 2.2 to compare examples of EQs and closed questions in elementary grades and to illustrate differences.

As Table 2.2 illustrates, essential questions encourage students to understand the "why" and "how" of disciplines to support, at the most basic level, why it is important to learn information in ELA, mathematics, social studies, and science. So often, students are highly attuned to the standards and how they connect to material that will be tested, which we agree is a realistic and necessary focus in today's elementary classrooms. Yet, disciplinary literacy, particularly in elementary grades, introduces students to the importance of school learning and how it can support a more democratic, analytical, and socially conscious world.

Do we expect a 1st-grader to study four advanced primary sources to draw a conclusion about an event in history? In one word, no. Our focus is on using disciplinary literacy extensions and frameworks to introduce young learners to different types of texts that are considered sources and how one source does not tell a complete story in history. An appropriate essential question in elementary grades might promote the idea that it is important to consider multiple historical sources and might help students organize their thinking when reading or viewing multiple texts. This will begin to introduce students to analysis of multiple sources as an important disciplinary concept in history.

Table 2.2. Essential Questions Versus Closed Questions

Discipline	Essential Questions	Closed Questions
English Language Arts	Why is point of view important?	Whose point of view is *Amazing Grace* told from?
Mathematics	How are estimates important in everyday life?	What is an estimation?
Social Studies	What makes something valuable? (economics) How do sources influence history? (history)	What is the value of a U.S. dime? Who wrote the Declaration of Independence?
Science	Why is it important to understand cause-and-effect relationships?	What happens when you place an ice cube in hot water?

Phase 2 in Practice

Returning to our elementary social studies example, an EQ such as, "Did Pocahontas save Captain John Smith's life?" may be beneficial to extend learning to include disciplinary literacy. This EQ invites students to investigate who both of these historical figures were and the circumstances in which they interacted, and to use information to make decisions about events related to the relationship of Pocahontas and Captain John Smith. This EQ implicitly promotes the study of multiple sources of information to draw a conclusion and provides an interesting lens through which students may approach the study of a well-known historical event that often is taught based solely on facts and dates, or references to a popular animated movie. Providing students with more than one source of information to address this question allows them a unique opportunity to engage in consideration of historical sources as well as learn about historical figures important to the early history of America.

PHASE 3:
SELECTING MULTIMODAL TEXTS FOR DISCIPLINARY LITERACY

As Shanahan and Shanahan (2014) describe, "The informational texts used in the elementary grades should represent a wide range of text types . . . modalities . . . and purposes. And through such texts elementary teachers can begin to prepare students for disciplinary reading by helping them distinguish among the texts" (p. 638). Phase 3 of the PEDDL Framework encourages teachers to first consider the texts currently used and their usefulness in the classroom context, and then extend instruction to include disciplinary literacy by selecting a variety of texts to: (a) expose students to distinctive features found across disciplinary texts, such as maps, speeches, photographs, shapes, or graphs, and (b) provide support for reading advanced texts by making them accessible to students with a range of reading abilities through the addition of audio and visual features. It is in this phase that we shift focus to the role of digital texts and tools to support disciplinary literacy. While we agree that print-based texts are highly valuable and necessary to disciplinary learning, we also encourage teachers to consider the distinct literacy capabilities of their elementary students.

Most elementary students, particularly in the early grades, are still developing their traditional reading skills, which often present a challenge when using disciplinary texts that present complex information or a format that differs from fiction literature that students may be more familiar with (Duke, 2000). Digital texts can act as a scaffold to engage students in disciplinary learning by presenting information in a format more understandable and relatable to young learners (Hutchison & Colwell, 2015).

Further, it is important, from a disciplinary perspective, to consider multiple sources of information when addressing a question or problem, so that various viewpoints can inform students' thinking to construct knowledge (Moje, 2015). We also see multitext selection as critical to extending students' thinking beyond the information found in traditional textbooks or readers, which often offer only one perspective. These texts also should represent multiple modalities or formats to accurately represent the types of texts that disciplinarians use in their studies (Moje, 2015).

Experts employ a range of texts, including images, graphics, and artifacts, in analysis. It is important, particularly at the elementary level, to expose students to the many types of texts that may be "read" and that are common to each discipline. Remember, reading and writing in disciplinary literacy, especially when supported by digital texts and tools, may look different depending on the text. The way that we read, or view, a digital image differs from the way we approach word-based text. This difference may be advantageous to students who struggle with traditional reading skills.

A variety of text types are also useful for helping students gain new knowledge and generate responses that demonstrate their understandings. We believe that multiple varieties of multimodal texts are essential to elementary literacy instruction, not only because digital texts provide unprecedented access to unique texts, artifacts, and experiences, but also because it is essential that students learn how to read, write, and communicate with digital texts in order to be fully literate (Dalton, 2012; Hutchison, Woodward, & Colwell, 2016). We also see this variety as critical to supporting multiple reading levels, as multimodal and/or digital texts often can scaffold students' reading with added graphics, audio, or video. To aid in disciplinary text selection, we encourage teachers to refer to Colwell's (2019) Disciplinary Text Selection Table (p. 633) created to support culturally responsive disciplinary literacy instruction (see Table 2.3).

We used this table as a starting point for considering text selection in elementary disciplines. In Chapters 3, 5, 7, and 9 we expand on each of the disciplines in this table to provide more concrete examples of multimodal and digital texts to consider.

Phase 3 in Practice

Returning to our history example, teachers might consider the existing print texts they use to explore colonial America and evaluate them for how they reflect disciplinary practices. In addition to, or in place of, these texts, elementary students who are still developing higher-level reading skills, which are often necessary to study historical word-based texts with archaic language, could compare digital artifacts from national museums that provide audio-based, kid-friendly summative explanations of written historical documents as well as digital images from the colonial period in American history. These types of digital texts provide students with multiple interpretations that may be consumed and comprehended more easily than print-based historical texts. These early acts of comparing historical texts, even in digital formats, is a foundational aspect of disciplinary literacy. Such digital texts, like documents and artifacts from museums focused on making such documents accessible to the public, would allow young learners an opportunity to engage in more independent analysis of text and would illuminate the importance of different perspectives when understanding historical events.

Table 2.3. The Disciplinary Text Selection Table

Discipline	Text Type Examples	Questions to Consider
English	Books (fiction and nonfiction) Essays Poems Short stories	• Am I selecting more than one text for students to compare literary topics, connections to inspired events, and time periods? • If I select only one text, does the message lend itself to multiple interpretations? Can it be compared with a previously studied text? • Do the texts represent a variety of literary, social, and/or cultural perspectives? • Are authors of minority backgrounds, genders, and cultures represented in the text selection? • Do the texts connect to one another so that students can draw comparisons? • What texts will students create to support English literacy?
History/ Social Studies	Artifacts Cartoons Documentaries Maps Photographs Paintings Primary documents Trade books	• Am I selecting more than one text for students to use in corroboration of historical information? • Am I selecting different types of historical texts, sources, and text formats? • Do the historical texts represent a variety of perspectives and voices? • Do the historical voices represented reflect cultures and backgrounds similar to those of my students? • What texts will students create to support historical literacy?

(table continues on next page)

Table 2.3. The Disciplinary Text Selection Table *(continued)*

Discipline	Text Type Examples	Questions to Consider
Mathematics	Charts Equations Formulas Graphs Proofs Symbols Shapes	• Does the text I selected represent an idea or problem grounded in mathematics that can connect to students' lives? • Can the text be used to solve or illustrate a socially or culturally relevant issue or problem in mathematics? • What additional text(s) might support the same mathematical idea or problem to provide additional perspectives on approaches or solutions? • What texts will students create to support mathematical literacy?
Science	Diagrams Graphs Lab reports Mathematical equations Photographs and images Proposals	• Do the texts I selected address a relevant science-focused issue in society? • Are the scientific perspectives represented in the texts varied in perspective and background? • Can the scientific data represented in the texts be connected to students' culture and backgrounds? • What texts will students create to support scientific literacy?

PHASE 4:
ASSESSING DISCIPLINARY LITERACY WITH A VARIETY OF TOOLS

Just as Phase 3 focused on digital texts, Phase 4 casts a keen look at digital tools that might be useful to understanding elementary students' learning of more advanced disciplinary literacy practices. While reviewing any existing assessments related to a particular standard of focus, it is important to consider how those assessments capture the complexity of student learning and the types of knowledge and understanding being evaluated. It may be that the existing assessments do not fully incorporate the disciplinary extensions of interest, and that a more robust assessment, such as a performance assessment, might better support student learning.

Performance Tasks

Grounded in foundations of backward design (Wiggins & McTighe, 2005) in planning instruction, we believe that students' "understanding is revealed in performance" (Wiggins & McTighe, 2005, p. 153), particularly in re-gard to disciplinary literacy where students are exploring texts, driven by a disciplinary EQ, to develop their own interpretations and conclusions. Additionally, performance tasks, or authentic learning tasks, ask students to engage in the subject through exploration similar to that of a disciplinarian (Wiggins & McTighe, 2005).

For example, performance tasks may include culminating assessments such as drafting a response to a government official describing a student's position on a current topic, or creating some type of model to represent understandings. These types of tasks ask students to consider their learning as a whole and apply that learning to an authentic task. For that reason, we highlight the planning of performance tasks as an essential component of the PEDDL Framework. After determining standards-based practices, creating EQs, and selecting a range of multimodal texts, teachers should think about comprehensive assessments that allow students to use and apply the knowledge they learn in the lesson. To define performance tasks in the PEDDL Framework, we relied on the following characteristics, as outlined by Wiggins and McTighe (2005, p. 153):

1. Involves a real or simulated real-world setting
2. Requires the student to address a real or simulated real-world audience
3. Is based on a purpose that would authentically relate to that audience
4. Allows students to personalize the task
5. Is given prior to learning so that the student's learning may be guided by the task

We do note here that although performance tasks are a critical part of the PEDDL Framework, we also value and support other types of assessment, such as informal or summative assessments or formal tests or writing, that provide teachers with an understanding of students' literacy learning. When helping teachers plan for disciplinary literacy in elementary grades, we offer a space for such assessments as well. However, we highlight the necessity of performance tasks to promote the use of disciplinary skills, par-ticularly tasks that provide students a digital platform with which to present their learning.

Particularly, digital tools provide all learners the opportunity to pres-ent their disciplinary learning in ways that are individual to each student. Digital tools offer support features, such as dictation, graphic represen-tation, video recording, and audio features, to name a few, that expand the ways in which young learners may communicate their understandings. These may be particularly useful if students engage in performance tasks that are writing intensive.

Phase 4 in Practice

Let's return to our example of having students study multiple sources of information to respond to the EQ, "Did Pocahontas save Captain John Smith's life?" As discussed previously, this question requires that students support their yes/no answers with evidence to explain their thinking and learning from their disciplinary study of this event in American history. Often in history, assessments involve students writing a word-based, essay-type response to such a question. However, we recognize that in elementary grades, students' understandings of their learning might be more complex than they can convey appropriately through a traditional, written, long-answer format. This phase of the PEDDL Framework promotes the use of digital tools to assess students' learning in order to more accurately gauge students' understanding.

For example, elementary students might use digital tools to create a digital storyboard focused on Pocahontas's role in Captain John Smith's rescue, using images and graphics, written and image-based text and/or audio, along with digital links to sources that support their interpretations of the sources they studied. To make the assessment authentic and for a real audience, teachers might frame the project as a presentation to a local museum or library that is planning an exhibit on this topic. Or, they may have students pretend to be Pocahontas or John Smith and digitally record what they learned using an avatar tool, such as Voki. Assessments such as these not only would address a number of traditional literacy skills, but also would support students in developing disciplinary literacy practices related to organizing and communicating information. In addition, this format allows for direct assessment of students' understanding of disciplinary literacy skills. For example, students also might address in a presentation why it was important to study multiple viewpoints and historical sources, and what they learned from different sources. This makes the assessment more comprehensive of students' understanding, bringing the assessment full circle to connect to real-world learning and skills.

PHASE 5:
DIGITALLY SUPPORTING DISCIPLINARY LITERACY INSTRUCTION

This phase represents the area of planning that teachers are most familiar with—the daily outline of activities and instructional techniques that will support students in learning the content at hand. The purpose of this phase is to bring together ideas from the first four phases to determine the specific lesson approach and consider the individual needs of students. Thus, this phase builds on teachers' existing instructional planning and knowledge related to supporting students' learning and comprehension, and engaging students in their own learning, and directly connects to students' individual needs and skills in disciplinary literacy to determine what literacy strategies and scaffolds are necessary to support students.

In particular, this phase encourages teachers to think about the types of strategies and digital tools that students will work with on a daily basis to engage their learning. Because Phase 3 and Phase 4 have already sparked thoughts on digital texts and tools, teachers likely have a preliminary idea for the digital component(s) of disciplinary literacy instruction. This phase provides a space to integrate the planning of standards and learning objectives, disciplinary practices and essential questions, texts, and assessments in the previous phases within the context of the particular needs of students in a classroom. It is during this phase that planning is designed related to the specific digital texts or tools that will be used, how they will be introduced, how often students will use them, and in what capacity this instruction will occur. Additionally, this phase is an opportunity to connect traditional and content-area literacy strategies to digital texts and tools so that students can be fully supported in their learning.

As we discussed in Chapter 1, students may benefit from using traditional and content-area literacy strategies to engage in disciplinary literacy practices, as those strategies can support readers who may struggle with or are unfamiliar with disciplinary texts (Brock et al., 2014; Faggella-Luby et al., 2012; Gillis, 2014; Hynd-Shanahan, 2013). Further, traditional literacy skills are a common thread in state and national standards. Thus, in elementary grades, integrating traditional and content-area literacy strategies may be necessary and useful to support a disciplinary literacy approach, as students are still shaping their reading skills with increasingly difficult informational texts.

We used a three-phase approach, common to content-area literacy instruction (see Alvermann, Gillis, & Phelps, 2012; Richardson, Morgan, & Fleener, 2012), to consider how disciplinary literacy practices might best be supported in instruction and to determine when and how content literacy strategies and digital texts and tools would be incorporated: (1) preparation for learning, (2) guiding learning, and (3) reflecting on learning. Using this approach, teachers consider the potential of digital tools for extending students' prior knowledge and preparing them to learn; identify digital tools that would serve to scaffold student learning, comprehension, and analysis of disciplinary texts; support students' ability to synthesize their learning across multiple text types; and contribute to the development of meaningful artifacts that demonstrate knowledge of the learning objective(s) and related disciplinary literacy practices.

Phase 5 in Practice

We return to our Pocahontas and John Smith example to illustrate this process. To prepare students for learning about disciplinary literacy practices, teachers should consider students' prior knowledge and look for ways to either activate knowledge that already exists or supplement or restructure knowledge that students might not yet have. Students might have existing knowledge about Pocahontas and John Smith from the popular Disney movie, but much of this movie is historically inaccurate. Thus, teachers might prepare students for learning by using a KWL (What I Want to Know, What I Know, and What I Learned) chart (Ogle, 1986) or an antic-ipation guide (Merkley, 1996/1997) to understand students' prior knowl-edge before beginning an analysis of the texts selected in Phase 3. These charts and guides can be in paper or digital format and still serve the pur-pose of helping teachers activate and understand students' prior knowl-edge. However, a teacher may find that digital KWL charts or anticipation guides might benefit students as they revise their initial views and add new information and perspectives. A digital document also might deepen students' preparation for historical disciplinary practices through students' analyzing one another's prior knowledge and considering multiple per-spectives as an introduction to multiple text analysis. It is in this prepara-tion phase as well that teachers may present sources so that students can begin to differentiate between primary and secondary historical sources, and may engage students in identifying sources to build their disciplinary knowledge of texts.

Teachers might guide students through disciplinary literacy by scaffold-ing their analysis of multiple texts. For young learners, especially, the act of reading across sources is challenging. However, digital texts and tools can lessen this challenge by providing students with (a) an organizational method to store their learning, and (b) a variety of texts suitable for their age and literacy levels. For example, students may use a digital graphic or-ganizer to store the digital texts presented on Pocahontas and John Smith and annotate with either doodles, drawings, or words to explain the im-portance and meaning of those texts. Importantly, these activities are akin to the approaches that historians take when navigating multiple complex documents, thus further contributing to developing students' understanding of disciplinary literacy practices.

While consideration of how students reflect on their disciplinary liter-acy learning takes place primarily in Phase 4 as part of determining per-formance-based assessments, Phase 5 allows teachers to map out how they might scaffold students' work in these assessments and provide strategies to support students' learning. For example, if students were to make a digital storyboard to depict the relationship between Pocahontas and John Smith during the time of colonial settlement in Virginia, teachers would need to determine how they would introduce a digital storyboard tool, the process for transferring students' learning to storyboards, and the level of support and opportunities for collaboration they would provide for students in this process of reflection.

Note that the examples we provided are a blend of traditional and digitally supported learning. Although we promote digital tools to scaffold and support students' learning during instruction, many different types of learning tools are available and useful for disciplinary literacy instruction. It is up to the teacher to determine when, where, and how students might best be supported with digital texts and tools. Specific examples situated within each of the four core disciplines are discussed in the subsequent chapters of this book.

PHASE 6: REFLECTING TO REACH ALL LEARNERS

We include a sixth and final phase in the PEDDL Framework to encourage elementary teachers to review, revisit, and reflect on their planned disciplinary literacy instruction supported by digital texts and tools. The final phase of the PEDDL Framework offers an opportunity for teachers to revisit their lesson or project in order to think about whether, in fact, standards, practices, texts, performance tasks, and instructional supports align with learning about the intended disciplinary literacy practices. Here we invite teachers to ground their reflection in the importance of developing personal, social, and cultural understandings in order to support students from all backgrounds.

We often include guiding questions in our teacher preparation courses and professional development as a way to support teachers in focusing on the essential elements of their instructional planning. For the purposes of reviewing and reflecting upon instruction planned using the PEDDL Framework, we present reflection questions that are tied specifically to a particular phase of planning and have created a checklist to use as a guide (see Figure 2.1).

We encourage teachers to revisit their text resources with a critical eye to determine whether the resources are both appropriate and challenging for students to use for digging deeper into disciplinary learning. This is where we see digital texts playing a large role in elementary disciplinary literacy, as digital texts offer multiple modalities that may better reach a variety of learners. Then, we ask teachers to consider students' outcomes on performance tasks and how disciplinary literacy may be assessed in these tasks. Next, we ask teachers to consider the traditional and content-area literacy approaches and whether those methods would support all students in reading the disciplinary texts. Lastly, when analyzing the final instructional plan, we invite teachers to specifically consider the needs of individual students in their class and how their instruction reflects aims related to personal, social, and cultural understandings.

Simply put, we included the sixth phase as a space for teachers to critically examine the digitally supported lesson/activity they developed and

Figure 2.1. Reflection to Reach All Learners Checklist

Phase 1: Identifying Appropriate Disciplinary Literacy Practices

— My disciplinary practices align with state standards and learning objectives.

— I have considered the personal, social, and cultural understandings that inform this lesson.

Phase 2: Framing Disciplinary Literacy

— I have identified essential questions that will promote meaningful understanding for students while fostering their growth toward specific learning goals and engaging them in disciplinary practices.

Phase 3: Selecting Multimodal Texts for Disciplinary Literacy

— I have reviewed the Disciplinary Text Selection Table (DTST) to identify possible types of texts within the discipline.

— The texts I have selected using the guiding questions within the DTST represent:

    — Important disciplinary texts

    — Multiple types of texts, including digital and multimodal texts

    — Culturally responsive texts

Phase 4: Assessing Disciplinary Literacy with a Variety of Tools

— I have identified the evidence needed to demonstrate student learning and progression toward understanding disciplinary practices.

— My selected digital tool(s) supports the disciplinary practice(s) I've chosen to target.

— I have provided students with authentic opportunities to create evidence that can be used to assess their learning.

Phase 5: Digitally Supporting Disciplinary Literacy Instruction

— I have considered the skills, knowledge, and understandings that my students will need in order to be successful in this lesson.

— I include specific instructional approaches that support students' comprehension of the multiple disciplinary texts selected for this lesson.

— I create opportunities for students to engage with the type and purpose of the text.

— My learning activities support students as they synthesize information through the analysis of multiple texts.

— I provide multiple opportunities for students to create authentic artifacts to show evidence of their learning.

Figure 2.1. Reflection to Reach All Learners Checklist *(continued)*

Phase 6: Reflecting to Reach All Learners

— My lesson plan is aligned among all of the planning phases to support students in their digitally supported disciplinary literacy growth.

— I return to review and reflect after the lesson to reflect on the teaching and learning that occurred, especially noting:

— Effective instructional approaches

— Useful digital tools for engaging students in meeting the learning objectives, in disciplinary practices, and in creating evidence

— Multimodal disciplinary texts that contributed to the synthesis of information

---

whether and how it will support disciplinary literacy for all learners in their classroom. In the following section, we offer an example of specific considerations that may emerge through reflection on the Pocahontas and John Smith lesson for diverse learners.

CONSIDERATIONS FOR DIVERSE LEARNERS IN THE PEDDL FRAMEWORK

We propose here explicitly, and implicitly throughout this book, that teachers consider that student populations, and the greater society, are made up of many different academic abilities, and cultural, racial, linguistic, and socioeconomic backgrounds, and that people learn in many different ways, at different rates, and with unique strengths and challenges. Planning for diverse learners, in our view, is to plan for instruction that is inclusive and encompassing of all students (Center for Applied Special Technology [CAST], 2019; Ladson-Billings, 2014; Moll, Amanti, Neff, & Gonzalez, 1992). This type of planning requires that teachers, throughout the PEDDL Framework, be aware of their students' particular needs and strengths, and also how to reach and engage all learners.

Moll and colleagues (1992), in their landmark work on culture and classroom practice, argued that all students come to school with their own specific "funds of knowledge," or skills and experiences, they have acquired through their homes and communities. Often this knowledge, particularly for cultural minorities, is overlooked in instruction as teachers focus on learning specific rules and facts. Yet, Moll and colleagues suggested that teachers should tap into students' funds of knowledge to make learning meaningful and to provide a method for culturally diverse students to highlight the knowledge they have, which sometimes is constrained by classroom activities. Although Moll and colleagues' argument is focused on students of different cultural backgrounds, the same concept applies to students with different learning needs, particularly students with disabilities, such as specific learning disabilities, autism spectrum disorder, intellectual disability, emotional and behavioral disorder, and communication disorder.

Most teachers likely will teach students with one or more of these disabilities at some point, given that 6.7 million children in the United States receive special education services (National Center for Education Statistics, 2018a). Similarly, many teachers will have students without diagnosed disabilities who simply have difficulty with reading or writing and require varying supports in the classroom. As with students from different cultural backgrounds, these students also have strengths that are not routinely highlighted or accessed in the classroom context. Thus, our approach to disciplinary literacy planning provides many opportunities for teachers, through the use of digital tools, to differentiate instruction and highlight strengths for students with a variety of needs.

When using the PEDDL Framework, we encourage teachers to explicitly consider the cultural and academic backgrounds and intellectual and social needs of students. In fact, we argue that a disciplinary approach to planning literacy instruction may offer important opportunities to deliberately connect to students' cultural backgrounds and intellectual differences.

For example, when selecting multimodal texts for disciplinary literacy instruction in Phase 3, teachers may focus on students' diverse backgrounds and offer different texts and perspectives relevant to multiple learners (Toppel, 2015). Selection of diverse and varied texts supports an inclusive community of learners and readers. Texts that offer multiple perspectives and even ask students to question more traditional textbook information not only encourage a critical lens for learning, but place value on minority or less focal viewpoints in classroom learning.

Consider our previous focal example of having students examine multiple sources of information related to whether, or to what extent, Pocahontas saved Captain John Smith's life. We discussed in Phase 3 how different types of texts and sources could be used to have students study across digital and traditional historical sources to form a response based in evidence, and in Phase 4, how demonstrating knowledge of the contributions of multiple sources is an important historical disciplinary literacy practice. It is important when selecting sources for a diverse population of learners that the sources are varied in authorship and perspective and that minority voices are present. Also, teachers can directly highlight how history textbooks often offer the perspective of the dominant culture at the time. This mini-lesson in analysis of multiple sources itself becomes important in helping students to understand that more than one viewpoint is necessary for a complete and less biased historical account.

The same example of Pocahontas and John Smith can be used to consider how to design instruction for students with varying learning needs and academic abilities. In planning, teachers should consider how to present material in a variety of ways, such as direct instruction on the topic, a video, or even a board game on Pocahontas and John Smith. Providing multiple ways to complete an assignment is also a useful way to highlight students' individual academic strengths and help students demonstrate their understanding (CAST, 2019), which can be explicitly supported with digital tools. For example, students may have the option to use a digital book creator tool to generate a book report or to create a video or presentation. It is essential to consider the range of students' needs and backgrounds at the planning phase to proactively support students rather than only responding reactively to omissions and challenges as they arise.

GENERAL IDEAS FOR PRACTICE

Finally, we note that the six phases are guidelines for planning. The framework draws on existing instructional considerations and supports teachers as they consider how to extend that instruction into developing elementary students' disciplinary literacy practices. These phases may serve as a support for adapting existing lessons, or as a structure to develop new instruction based on existing objectives. In the case of the latter, we provide an instructional planning template in Appendix E online that organizes the phases and principles of the PEDDL Framework to support teachers in developing new instruction. Free printable PDF files for Appendices A–E are available online on the TCPress website: tcpress.com/colwell-app. Appendix E is also available as a Microsoft Word file.

This more structured approach to planning may be useful as teachers become familiar with planning for digitally supported disciplinary literacy. However, as this planning approach is used more frequently and teachers become more accustomed to this planning, a less formal approach may be more appropriate. At times, teachers may choose to focus on one or two phases in particular, and focal phases may change as curricular topics change throughout the school year; this does not require a structured template such as Appendix E. However, we offer this template in an attempt to structure the PEDDL Framework in a format that can be used with any of the disciplinary literacy Core Disciplinary Practices discussed in the subsequent chapters. For illustration, we use the template in the additional lesson plans in Appendices A–D online for each of the disciplines that we discuss in the "Practical Approaches" chapters (Chapters 4, 6, 8, and 10).

CHAPTER 3

Examining Disciplinary Literacy in Elementary English Language Arts

Ms. Branch's students are beginning a poetry unit. Her school district utilizes the Common Core State Standards as its standards document, and she has identified the 3rd-grade Reading Literature standards to guide her instruction. Although she has taught this unit in previous years, this year she wants to challenge her students to not only create individual poems but analyze poetry to emphasize structure and patterns, and then create poetry using a similar format. As she is selecting the particular standard that will guide her instruction about poetry, she sees that one standard foregrounds disciplinary vocabulary in the context of engaging and analyzing text:

> Refer to parts of stories, dramas, and poems when writing or speaking about a text, using terms such as chapter, scene, and stanza; describe how each successive part builds on earlier sections. (CCSS.ELA-Literacy. RL.3.5)

Ms. Branch circles the words "Refer to," "using terms," and "describe" as key elements that represent ELA disciplinary literacy practices. She recognizes that these relate to the Core Disciplinary Practices of using vocabulary and communication. She begins to consider learning objectives, print texts, and digital materials that will support her students in understanding the discipline-specific vocabulary of ELA and how to use that vocabulary to discuss and share supported opinions about poetry.

INTEGRATING DISCIPLINARY LITERACY INTO ELA

English language arts is somewhat complex to navigate from an elementary disciplinary literacy perspective because much of K–5 ELA focuses on traditional literacy and making connections between ELA and other disciplines, given the prominent role reading and learning to read play in elementary ELA instruction and testing. Yet, ELA experts use a unique set of practices, often linked with higher level reading and comprehension abilities, and these practices are associated with disciplinary literacy. Further, these practices are targeted in recent elementary learning standards, which increases their importance in K–5 instruction and requires a closer look at how disciplinary literacy in ELA might be integrated into the elementary grades.

Who Are English Experts and What Do They Practice?

As we have discussed previously, foundations of disciplinary literacy are linked to the specific practices experts in a discipline use to study and think (Shanahan & Shanahan, 2008, 2012). Experts in the discipline of English often are considered to be English or literary scholars who study literature, both fiction and nonfiction, although journalists, writers, and editors also could be considered experts in English. Disciplinary literacy in ELA entails the practices those scholars use in their work with reading, analyzing, and communicating ideas about literature. These experts engage with texts in unique ways to construct knowledge that often addresses social issues. Rainey (2016) suggested that literary experts engage in a number of shared disciplinary practices, including:

- Exploring patterns across texts
- Identifying and examining strange or surprising aspects of text
- Developing interpretive literary puzzles
- Considering the historical, cultural, and social context of a text
- Making original text-based claims

These practices indicate that experts read across texts to seek similarities or connections between texts. They also consider strange or surprising parts of literary texts that might hold additional meaning. In doing so, English scholars build puzzles by questioning these strange or surprising parts to connect them back to the larger work of literature. To inform their interpretations, often scholars also think about when the text was written and in what circumstances. Finally, they make claims about the text they analyzed, based on their literary interpretations (Rainey, 2016).

Yet, other scholars aptly argue that composition and linguistics are critical English practices as well (Smagorinsky, 2015). Indeed, journalists, poets, and writers of various genres of fiction and nonfiction would be considered English experts as well, adding composition and linguistics to the ELA disciplinary literacy. Table 3.1 connects these combined expert practices to the Core Disciplinary Practices of focus in this book.

Note that Table 3.1 does not encompass all ELA expert practices discussed previously, as we selected only practices that are appropriate for elementary learners. For example, most elementary students would struggle with advanced practices such as considering the historical, cultural, or social context of literature during analysis. However, elementary students can read

Table 3.1. Connections Between Expert and Core ELA Practices

ELA Expert Practices	Core Disciplinary Practices
• Exploring patterns across texts • Identifying and examining strange or surprising aspects of text	• Recognizing or comprehending multiple types of text • Analysis across multiple texts
• Making original text-based claims	• Comprehending and using vocabulary particular to a discipline • Developing and communicating ideas, arguments, or rationalizations
• Composing creative or informational texts	• Developing and communicating ideas, arguments, or rationalizations

texts closely for patterns, think about elements of literature that are surprising, and make claims based on what they read or viewed using vocabulary particular to ELA, placing an emphasis on analysis of text. Also, students write various types of texts to express ideas in elementary ELA, highlighting the role of communication in K–5 English.

What Role Do Digital Tools Play in Expert English Practices?

When thinking about digitally supported disciplinary literacy, it can be useful to consider the kinds of digital tools commonly used by English experts. Many of the same tools can be used by students in elementary grades, although in more simplistic ways. A look at the tools of experts also can prompt teachers to consider the types of tasks that experts undertake with these tools. Teachers can help students develop the digital literacy skills they may need to use these digital tools. Table 3.2 outlines some of these tools by area of expertise, with connections to the types of tools that might be supportive of disciplinary literacy in English language arts learning.

What Standards Promote ELA Disciplinary Literacy?

To address a wide audience, we focus on connecting national or professional standards to each core discipline's practices. For ELA, we turn to the Common Core State Standards. These standards have been adopted by and serve as language-related benchmarks for 41 U.S. states. Further, many of the states that did not adopt the CCSS, such as Virginia, have formally outlined how their state standards align with the CCSS, recognizing similar and compatible goals. Like Ms. Branch did, we take a look at disciplinary practices and foci outlined in the ELA CCSS.

Table 3.2. Expert Digital Tool Connections

Experts	Professional Digital Tools	Possibilities for Classroom Application
Writers (literary or technical)	• Cloud-based system for saving and sharing documents • Word processing tools • Collaborative-writing tools for co-authoring content • Digital databases for research • Websites or social media accounts for promoting writing or showcasing portfolio of work • Tools for creating images and videos • Digital tools for drafting and planning content • Automated editing software	• Locating, evaluating, synthesizing, and communicating information from online resources • Saving and sharing digital files • Collaborative writing with Google Docs or similar tool • Evaluating the content of social media posts • Creating content for social media posts • Creating powerful images to supplement words • Graphic organizers for planning content
Editors	• Cloud-based system for saving and sharing documents • Word processing software or website • Digital editing tools • Spreadsheets for tracking projects • Automated editing software	• Saving and sharing digital files • Editing digital documents • Sharing feedback through digital sites such as Google Docs
Social Media Content Writers or Managers	• Social media sites • Digital camera • Digital video recorder • Spreadsheets for planning content • Automated editing software • Infographic creators	• Evaluating the content of social media posts • Creating content for social media posts • Creating multimodal messages • Creating persuasive infographics

Table 3.3 highlights sample standards that reflect how disciplinary literacy has emerged in each of the elementary grades, beginning in kindergarten. Within the ELA CCSS, the standards are organized broadly into reading standards related to literature (abbreviated in the CCSS as RL), informational text (RI), foundational skills (RF), writing (W), speaking and listening

Table 3.3. ELA Standards and Disciplinary Literacy Practices

Grade Level	ELA CCSS
K	**CCSS.ELA-Literacy.RL.K.5** **Recognize** common **types of texts** (e.g., storybooks, poems). **CCSS.ELA-Literacy.W.K.7** **Participate in shared research and writing** projects (e.g., explore a number of books by a favorite author and **express opinions** about them).
1	**CCSS.ELA-Literacy.RL.1.5** **Explain major differences** between books that tell stories and books that give information, **drawing on a wide reading** of a range of text types. **CCSS.ELA-Literacy.W.1.1** **Write opinion pieces** in which they introduce the topic or name the book they are writing about, **state an opinion, supply a reason** for the opinion, and **provide** some sense of **closure.**
2	**CCSS.ELA-Literacy.RL.2.9** **Compare and contrast** two or more versions of the same story (e.g., Cinderella stories) by different authors or from different cultures. **CCSS.ELA-Literacy.W.2.3** **Write narratives** in which they **recount** a well-elaborated event or short sequence of events, include details to **describe** actions, thoughts, and feelings, **use temporal words to signal** event order, and provide a sense of closure.

(SL), and language (L). Table 3.3 focuses on example standards from each grade, while Chapter 4 expands upon the breadth of ELA standards in K–5 instruction. We note in bold the action-oriented and discipline-focused language of these standards that encourage disciplinary literacy, rather than passive reading or writing.

While all ELA standards are designed to support the literacy learning of students, not all standards may contribute to an understanding of the disciplinary literacy practices in ELA. Indeed, as shown in Table 3.3, teachers may need to break down a standard to identify specific components that can contribute to an understanding of disciplinary literacy. Identifying the particular parts of a standard that contribute to disciplinary literacy knowledge can support student learning of the disciplinary literacy practices alongside the broader ELA standard.

Table 3.3. ELA Standards and Disciplinary Literacy Practices *(continued)*

Grade Level	ELA CCSS
3	**CCSS.ELA-Literacy.RL.3.5** **Refer** to parts of stories, dramas, and poems when writing or speaking about a text, **using terms** such as chapter, scene, and stanza; **describe** how each successive part builds on earlier sections.
4	**CCSS.ELA-Literacy.RL.4.9** **Compare and contrast** the treatment of similar themes and topics (e.g., opposition of good and evil) and **patterns** of events (e.g., the quest) in stories, myths, and traditional literature from different cultures. **CCSS.ELA-Literacy.W.4.1** **Write** opinion pieces on topics or texts, supporting a point of view **with reasons and information.**
5	**CCSS.ELA-Literacy.RL.5.1** **Quote accurately** from a text when explaining what the text says explicitly and when **drawing inferences** from the text. **CCSS.ELA-Literacy.W.5.2.D** **Use** precise **language and domain-specific vocabulary** to inform about or explain the topic.

Selecting ELA Texts for Disciplinary Literacy Instruction

Selecting appropriate ELA texts to use in disciplinary literacy instruction is one of the first important steps in planning. As we discussed in Chapter 2, texts, from a disciplinary perspective, can encompass a myriad of items that can be read, viewed, or consumed (Draper & Siebert, 2010). One need not be limited solely to books or print-based reading materials when considering ELA disciplinary literacy instruction. A variety of texts is important to expose students to multiple definitions of text, which is a critical foundational skill in elementary disciplinary literacy (Shanahan & Shanahan, 2014).

Not only is it important to select a variety of texts for students to consider, but it is equally important to select texts that are culturally and linguistically responsive (Colwell, 2019). We expand on Colwell's (2019) original Disciplinary Text Selection Table (p. 633) for elementary grades in Table 3.4 by noting digital, as well as traditional, texts useful for disciplinary literacy instruction, and questions for consideration in selecting these texts. The DTST was developed originally as a framework for elementary teachers to select culturally responsive texts in the disciplines. The questions can be used as prompts to support text selection.

Table 3.4. Modified Disciplinary Literacy Text Selection for ELA

Print, Digital, and Other Multimodal Text Types	Questions to Consider
Picture books (digital and nondigital/fiction and nonfiction) Essays Poems Short stories Audiobooks/ recorded poetry or songs Videos Websites Curated digital content Digital and nondigital leveled books	• Am I selecting more than one text for students to compare literary topics, connections to inspired events, and time periods? • Am I selecting multimodal texts that can support a variety of learner levels? • If I select only one text, does the message lend itself to multiple interpretations? Can it be compared with a previously studied text? Is that text available in multiple formats to increase readability (e.g., animated, auditory)? • Do the texts represent a variety of literary, social, and/ or cultural perspectives? • Are authors of minority backgrounds, genders, and cultures represented in the text selection? • Do the texts connect to one another so that students can draw comparisons? • What texts will students create to support literacy skills in ELA? • What texts will support students who may struggle with ELA practices?

As Table 3.4 suggests, the types of texts teachers select directly influence connections to culture, language, and society, and relevant aspects of disciplinary literacy. Table 3.4 also emphasizes the importance of considering a variety of texts to support an array of learners and ability levels in an elementary classroom. Finally, through both the example texts and questions, Table 3.4 highlights the contributions of different types of digital and traditional texts to students' understanding of ELA disciplinary literacy practices.

HOW CAN DISCIPLINARY LITERACY INSTRUCTION BE DIGITALLY SUPPORTED IN ELA?

Although multiple reasons exist to incorporate disciplinary literacy practices into ELA instruction, elementary teachers, in general, have had little training or preparation in doing so (Fisher, 2019; Shanahan & Shanahan, 2014). Further, these practices may be more advanced and require scaffolding for all learners to engage in them. Here, we focus on two methods for considering this integration in connection with the Core Disciplinary Practices in this book. In the following chapter, we will put these methods into action through sample lessons.

First, we highlight content literacy strategies that can serve as scaffolds for organizing students' thinking and approaches to reading and writing in the disciplines. Indeed, recent literature encourages teachers to consider how content literacy strategies might support disciplinary literacy, and considers the potential of using such strategies in disciplinary literacy instruction (Dunkerly-Bean & Bean, 2016; Gillis, 2014; Hynd-Shanahan, 2013). Second, we suggest digital tools that might support the Core Disciplinary Practices in ELA, as digital tools hold much potential for supporting all learners in disciplinary literacy and may aid students in engaging in practices somewhat advanced for their grade or ability level.

So often, a singular focus in elementary ELA is fiction, particularly in a print-based story format. While we agree that fiction stories are key texts in English language arts, we argue that to be prepared for studying in the discipline of English, students must become familiar with multiple types of texts that are useful in studying ELA. In particular, including informational texts may better prepare elementary students for more advanced reading in content areas and for the types of texts that typically are read in everyday life (Hedin & Conderman, 2010; Yopp & Yopp, 2012). Further, providing students with a wide variety of text formats, both traditional and digital, exposes students to different text types and often provides learners with multiple paths in which they may comprehend and compare information, which reflects authentic disciplinary literacy practices within ELA.

Recognizing and Comprehending Multiple Types of ELA Texts

Table 3.5 outlines sample literacy strategies and digital tools that might be used to support recognition and comprehension of multiple types of ELA texts. Notice the common instructional topic of these examples (i.e., fairy-tales) and how the use of strategies and tools builds from basic to more advanced as the grade levels increase. This is intentional to highlight how digitally supported disciplinary literacy instruction will differ among elementary ELA grade levels.

Analyzing ELA Texts

From a disciplinary literacy perspective, ELA instruction focuses heavily on text analysis. In elementary grades, this type of analysis often is referred to as close reading (Fisher & Frey, 2012). An important requirement of the CCSS, close reading engages students in critical analysis and searching for patterns within literature (both fiction and nonfiction texts) to create

Table 3.5. Literacy Strategies to Support Recognition and Comprehension of Multiple Types of ELA Texts

Grade Level	Literacy Strategy	Digital Tool	Example
K	Preview	Video clip	Students view a short *Three Little Pigs* video before reading the story for comparison.
2	List, group, label	Digital graphic organizer	After previewing different types of Cinderella stories (e.g., examining book jackets or viewing a video preview), students categorize/organize common features across texts using a digital graphic organizer that supports inclusion of graphics and text.
4	Anticipation guide	Screencast	Students preview two versions (text and digital) of *Alice's Adventures in Wonderland* to predict differences and similarities of the versions. They then create a digital representation and accompanying screencast to generate a multimodal narrative explaining their predictions, which they can confirm or disconfirm after reading/viewing.

meaning. During close reading, students read literature multiple times to understand character motives or how a text compares to other similar texts, to their lives, or sometimes to historical or current social issues. Although close reading can be considered a general strategic approach to text analysis (Fisher & Frey, 2012), many students will need additional support in close reading of multiple texts in ELA. Table 3.6 suggests strategies and tools that may be useful in this process.

Using Vocabulary Particular to ELA

Learning about disciplinary vocabulary in ELA supports students in understanding the disciplinary language related to recognizing and comprehending, analyzing, and communicating about texts. Supporting students in understanding the specific words and language that are used to describe literature, and how those words and language may be similar to and different from those used to describe informational texts, is a critical part of vocabulary instruction in ELA (Smagorinsky, 2015). It is important to note that

Table 3.6. Literacy Strategies to Support Analysis of ELA Texts

Grade Level	Literacy Strategy	Digital Tool	Example
1	Paired retelling	Digital autobiography Audio recorder	Students are partnered together and take turns reading/viewing an autobiography, alternating between coach and reader roles. Each pair has a different autobiography. Students then take turns retelling the information they read, while recording themselves. Retellings are shared among the class so that students can consider multiple retellings of autobiographical information.
3	Annotation	Digital annotation tool	Students read/view two texts, provided in digital formats, on a public figure. Students make audio or text annotations, using a digital annotation tool to hold their thinking or pose questions about text, that they can compare across texts after completing their readings.
5	Inquiry chart	Digital chart	Students read/view multiple informational texts on a public figure. Students fill out the digital chart, posing questions about the different texts, summarizing what they have learned in each text, and noting interesting facts. The digital chart allows students to link information to Internet resources, and it allows students who struggle with writing to use audio and illustrative features to capture thinking.

the vocabulary we refer to here is reflective of those words that are key to understanding English disciplinary practices, not context-dependent terms whose definitions must be provided to or found by students to make sense of a particular text. Rather, we focus on the specialized vocabulary that relates to figurative language, composition, and the analysis and discussion of literature and informational text.

Table 3.7. Literacy Strategies to Support ELA Vocabulary Instruction

Grade Level	Literacy Strategy	Digital Tool	Example
K	Interactive read-aloud	Video conferencing tool Digital video	Invite a guest author or play a recording of an author reading a story, pausing for students to orally discuss and ask/answer plot-related questions.
2	Four square	Digital graphic organizer	Students can use a digital four square–type organizer to illustrate four different things they know about plot through graphic representation, audio recording, etc.
4	Possible sentences	Google Docs	Give students plot-related terms to consider prior to reading a story. Students can collaboratively generate possible sentences in a Google Doc prior to reading, working together in small groups or partners to formulate sentences that might make sense in the context of the story. After reading, students can revisit the Google Doc as a class and edit or confirm their sentences based on their learning.

To exemplify approaches to supporting student learning of specialized disciplinary vocabulary, Table 3.7 shows how digitally supported literacy strategies can be used to support ELA instruction in vocabulary regarding plot characteristics in fiction.

Communicating in ELA

Developing the ability to communicate an opinion about a text and support an argumentative claim with evidence is an important disciplinary literacy practice in ELA (Rainey, 2016; Smagorinsky, 2015). Students should be engaged in different types of communication within their ELA classrooms, including speaking and discussing, listening, and writing in a variety of modes and genres. These opportunities can be grounded in a response to a particular disciplinary text or the teacher can select a traditional or digital anchor text to serve as a model for students' writing. Communicating about texts and creating texts serve to support students' in-the-moment recognition and comprehension, analysis, and vocabulary learning, and is also critical as an approach to synthesis and reflection after engaging with text, or post-reading. The post-reading approach is unique to the disciplinary literacy practice of communicating a rationalization in ELA and challenges teachers to reconceptualize traditional writing and communication practices. Table 3.8 focuses on ways students can be supported in developing and communicating a rationalization in ELA after reading multiple literary texts focused on the same theme.

Table 3.8. Literacy Strategies to Communicate in ELA

Grade Level	Literacy Strategy	Digital Tool	Example
1	Exit slip	Online response tool	Using an online response tool, such as Socrative, students informally suggest connections between a poem and a story using text and emojis/graphics to support their connections. Exit slips are sent directly to the teacher for individual and immediate feedback.
3	Summarizing	Podcast	As 3rd-graders' ability to create an argument might exceed their writing skills, students can orally summarize literary connections through an audio-recorded podcast that can be shared through a class blog or with partners at listening stations.
5	RAFT	Digital film	Students can use the RAFT (Role, Audience, Format, Topic) activity to present connections from the perspective of a character or figure. Students can create a video expressing their perspective and rationalization, based on text-based claims. Videos can be shared among the class or with other 5th-grade classes for comparison.

CHAPTER 4

Practical Approaches to Digitally Supported Disciplinary Literacy in ELA

In this and the other "Practical Approaches" chapters (6, 8, and 10), we provide detailed discussions of how to use the PEDDL Framework to plan instruction in real classroom contexts. These chapters address the particular discipline-related elements of planning digitally supported disciplinary literacy instruction, as well as provide concrete examples of lessons and considerations for planning related to each phase of the PEDDL Framework. While the lessons in these chapters may be adapted for use in a classroom, we also intend for them to serve as broad exemplars to inform the development of disciplinary literacy lessons for elementary grades. Each "Practical Approaches" chapter will focus on a different discipline and will demonstrate how to plan a disciplinary literacy lesson, in a particular grade, using the PEDDL Framework with detailed description of planning each phase. Additionally, we will introduce at the end of each "Practical Approaches" chapter, and provide in online appendices, a second lesson in a different grade level using the PEDDL Lesson Plan Template. We do so in an attempt to provide comprehensive examples in two different formats.

SAMPLE LESSON: EXAMINING CULTURALLY DIVERSE FAIRYTALES THROUGH LITERARY TEXT ANALYSIS IN 2ND GRADE

While all of the Core Disciplinary Practices are used in each discipline, we have noticed a substantial number of standards that specifically address a literary approach to understanding texts. That is, standards with a focus on practices such as exploring patterns across texts, identifying and examining strange or surprising aspects of text, and making original text-based claims reflect the ELA expert practices identified in the previous chapter. In light of these standards, we developed ELA lessons to focus on *analyzing text*. Additionally, as we developed this chapter, we kept in mind that ELA is the primary discipline of focus for traditional reading and writing skill development at the elementary level. Thus, in this particular discipline and chapter, we attempt to incorporate both disciplinary and traditional literacy skills as a focus in planning, as we feel this aligns with the reality of planning ELA instruction in elementary grades.

Phase 1: Identifying Appropriate Disciplinary Literacy Practices

Phase 1 (see Table 4.1) of the PEDDL Framework involves the selection of a Core Disciplinary Practice using existing learning standards and lesson objectives. For example, an existing 2nd-grade unit might involve ELA standards related to comparing and contrasting, as well as foundational literacy skills such as reading with purpose, understanding, and fluency. However, analyzing the standards with ELA disciplinary practices as a focus would highlight the potential within the compare and contrast standard to not only identify patterns across texts, but also recognize and explore interesting and surprising differences in the text. Further, electing to compare and contrast two stories that have different authors and cultures, rather than focusing on one or the other, likely would expose students to more-robust differences related to language, content, and cultural knowledge than only a switch of perspective or setting would.

In this case, the 2nd-grade lesson plan represents standards already used in a classroom, with only a change in the focus of the standards. The lesson objectives reflect the change in focus on the literature standard to include both different authors and cultures (CCSS.ELA-Literacy.RL.2.9), and refinement of the foundational skill of reading with purpose (CCSS.ELA-Literacy.RF.2.4.A), while maintaining the fluency-related objective (CCSS.ELA-Literacy.RF.2.4.B). Thus, we attempted in this lesson to balance required instruction in literacy skills with complementary disciplinary skills focused on text analysis.

Phase 2: Framing Disciplinary Literacy

Here, it is important to consider the existing ELA learning and understanding that typically happen with a particular lesson or unit and then extend that beyond what students are learning into *why* they are learning it. To support students' ELA disciplinary literacy skills, it is necessary to examine the disciplinary practices that inform understandings and the essential questions that support critical text analysis (see Table 4.1).

While it is important that students have the skills to compare and contrast different narratives, expertise in the ELA discipline involves an understanding of why recognizing and examining patterns and unexpected elements of text are essential. We argue that this understanding is essential for both disciplinary literacy and to support students in instruction that focuses on examination of differences in written text, which is a critical skill

(text continues on page 58)

Table 4.1. Planning Outline

Current Instructional Considerations	Disciplinary Extensions
PHASE 1: Identifying Appropriate Disciplinary Literacy Practices	
What state/national standards am I targeting?	What Core Disciplinary Practice is supported by those standards and objectives?
CCSS.ELA-Literacy.RL.2.9 Compare and contrast two or more versions of the same story (e.g., Cinderella stories) by different authors or from different cultures.	Analyzing text
CCSS.ELA-Literacy.RF.2.4.A Read grade-level text with purpose and understanding.	
CCSS.ELA-Literacy.RF.2.4.B Read grade-level text orally with accuracy, appropriate rate, and expression on successive readings.	
What are my lesson objectives?	
1. Students will read and compare and contrast two fairytales.	
2. Students will be able to orally read two fairytales with accuracy, appropriate rate, and expression.	
What are my revised lesson objectives after adding a Core Disciplinary Practice?	
1. Students will be able to recognize and analyze patterns across three culturally different stories.	
2. Students will be able to understand and examine stories for unexpected elements of text.	
3. Students will be able to read a story at their individual fluency goal.	

Table 4.1. Planning Outline *(continued)*

Current Instructional Considerations	Disciplinary Extensions
PHASE 2: Framing Disciplinary Literacy	
What information is important for my students to learn and understand from this lesson? 1. Literature is culturally influenced. 2. Commonalities exist across different cultures human experiences. 3. Perspective is highly important to the study of literature.	Why is it important for students to learn and understand this topic? Through focusing on stories that may be familiar to students, and asking them to re-examine those stories through the lens of another culture, students are better prepared to recognize the limitations of only one point of view, while also learning about archetypes that exist in literature around the world. What essential question(s) might frame the importance of understanding this topic? 1. Why are different perspectives important? 2. What kinds of experiences do humans have in common?
PHASE 3: Selecting Multimodal Texts for Disciplinary Literacy	
What texts does my school or school district require when teaching this topic? *Little Red Riding Hood* print-based text What texts do I feel comfortable using to support students' learning? Which topical texts align with my students' current reading levels? • *Little Red Riding Hood* [leveled PDF text available from Reading A–Z: www.readinga-z.com/book.php?id=2533] • *Petite Rouge: A Cajun Red Riding Hood* (Artell, 2001) [multimodal available at: youtu.be/eTswiDuwVL0] • *Lon Po Po: A Red-Riding Hood Story from China* (Young, 2016), [teacher read-aloud]	What digital and multimodal texts might supplement my currently used texts and extend students' learning to encourage disciplinary literacy? • Audio versions of the various Little Red Riding Hood stories • YouTube videos of readings/presentations of the various Little Red Riding Hood stories How might these digital and multimodal texts help support students to engage in more advanced reading, writing, and communication practices? These texts might allow students to read multiple texts in a shorter span of time and with more multimodal support to appropriately comprehend information, which in turn can be useful for more critical analysis.

(table continues on next page)

Table 4.1. Planning Outline *(continued)*

Current Instructional Considerations	Disciplinary Extensions
PHASE 4: Assessing Disciplinary Literacy with a Variety of Tools	
What assessments do I currently use to determine students' learning and understanding of this topic?	How can I incorporate digital tools to further assess students' understanding of disciplinary practices and texts?
• Graphic organizer or written assessment focused on story comprehension and comparison between two versions of a fairytale	Students can use a digital graphic organizer and then record oral discussion, either independently or in pairs, of their response to the essential questions on a graphic organizer and post to their Google Classroom for the teacher to listen to.
• Using leveled text to assess students' rate, accuracy, and prosody in reading	How do these digital tools create or support a more comprehensive assessment of students' understanding?
What type(s) of knowledge (e.g., fact-based, process-based, etc.) do those assessments gauge?	Because students read or consumed each of the texts in various formats, providing them an assessment in which they can orally discuss their analysis and conclusions may support a more robust assessment of students' analysis. Also, the teacher can more feasibly assess oral recordings than by having students orally explain their understandings during class.
• Understanding, comparison, and analysis of story elements, such as setting, main characters, and plot	
• Traditional reading skills	
PHASE 5: Digitally Supporting Disciplinary Literacy Instruction	
How do I prepare my students to learn this topic?	What digital tools extend and deepen students' preparation to learn this topic?
• Establish prior knowledge by having students independently read (and record their readings of) leveled text at Reading A–Z (www.readinga-z.com/book.php?id=2533).	• The teacher can introduce students to using digital graphic organizer tools and audio tools in Google Classroom.
• Prepare students for listening/viewing *Petite Rouge* and *Lon Po Po* by explaining that the structure will be the same, while the characters, setting, and plot may be different.	• Then, teacher and students can collaboratively create a plot diagram of *Little Red Riding Hood* using Storyboard That (www.storyboardthat.com/articles/e/plot-diagram) in order to serve as a reference point for the foundational story.
	• Utilize the plot diagram of *Little Red Riding Hood* to review the structure of a fairytale and the predictable patterns related to that genre.

Table 4.1. Planning Outline *(continued)*

Current Instructional Considerations	Disciplinary Extensions
PHASE 5: Digitally Supporting Disciplinary Literacy Instruction *(continued)*	

• Discuss why it is difficult to know the exact, original author of *Little Red Riding Hood*. Ask students what other stories they know and whether they know who wrote them. Discuss why different people might know different stories.	**What digital tools can I incorporate to scaffold students' disciplinary comprehension?**
	Integrate a digital concept mapping tool to identify the author, purpose of the story, and intended audience for both *Petite Rouge* and *Lon Po Po*.
How do I guide my students' comprehension of this topic?	**How do I help my students reflect on their learning of this topic?**
Provide graphic organization scaffolds to store interpretations and key plot elements of each story.	Students can add to the original class storyboard to highlight commonalities and discrepancies among the three texts, creating a collaborative final product that showcases their analysis of the texts.
How do I help my students reflect on their learning of this topic?	
After listening to *Petite Rouge* and *Lon Po Po*, engage in whole-class discussion with students to consider how they knew those texts were fairytales and to review basic plot elements of each. They can refer to their original storyboard of *Little Red Riding Hood* as a resource.	**What digital tools support students' development of artifacts to illustrate disciplinary literacy?**
	The storyboard will illustrate disciplinary literacy learning by providing a multimodal representation of text analysis.

PHASE 6: Reflecting to Reach All Learners	
How have I differentiated instruction in this lesson?	**How have I considered personal, social, and cultural understandings that inform this lesson?**
• Provided leveled versions of *Little Red Riding Hood*	Integrating different cultural versions of *Little Red Riding Hood* not only presents a culturally varied approach to reading a classic fairytale, but also provides students a window to understand perspective and how culture plays a role in literary interpretation. Providing different versions of this fairytale, along with multiple ways to read and present learning, also fosters more personal connections to learning.
• Provided a variety of modes for students to consume *Lon Po Po* and *Petite Rouge*	

for engaged citizenship. Indeed, exploring the personal, social, and cultural understandings that can be gained from reading literature, and using those to inform essential questions that support ELA disciplinary knowledge, can reveal useful insights into ELA disciplinary literacy and its value in real-world skills. Refer to the EQs planned for this lesson:

1. Why are different perspectives important?
2. What are experiences that humans have in common?

As illustrated through these questions, we encourage teachers to articulate how ELA disciplinary literacy instruction might be framed through students' understandings about multiple perspectives and cultural differences. In turn, we propose that teachers use those understandings as goals related to the essential questions that guide the lesson. By doing so, teachers maintain the existing knowledge typical of 2nd-grade instruction and subsequently extend it into ELA disciplinary literacy knowledge. However, we also tie foundational literacy skills, such as fluency, into instruction in ELA at the elementary level to help students understand why it is critical that they practice reading.

Phase 3: Selecting Multimodal Texts for Disciplinary Literacy

While all disciplines have a variety of text genres, ELA disciplinary practices reflect a wide range of text types (see Table 3.4 on p. 46). Selecting multimodal texts for use in elementary disciplinary literacy instruction may be made more difficult due to the sheer volume of texts in any particular genre of instruction. Following a selection process, such as Figure 4.1 outlines, may be beneficial to appropriate text selection.

For example, a 2nd-grade teacher typically might pair the text *The Three Little Pigs* with *The True Story of the Three Little Pigs* (Scieszka & Smith, 1996) to compare and contrast the same story from different points of view. When analyzing these currently used texts, the teacher might notice

Figure 4.1. The Text Selection Process

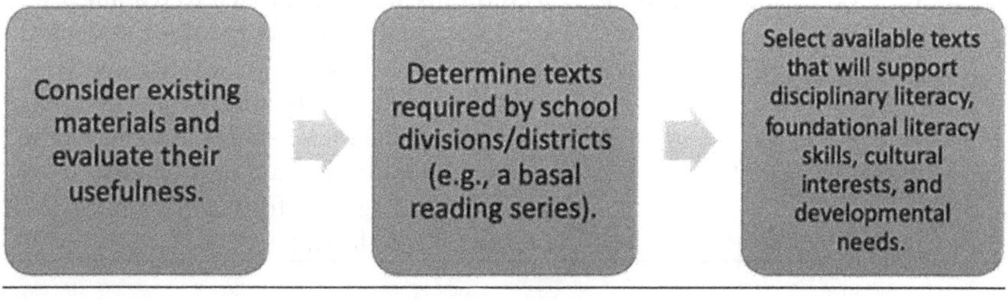

Consider existing materials and evaluate their usefulness. ⇒ Determine texts required by school divisions/districts (e.g., a basal reading series). ⇒ Select available texts that will support disciplinary literacy, foundational literacy skills, cultural interests, and developmental needs.

that the characters, plot, and much of the setting are the same; the primary difference between the two versions is the point of view. While this certainly satisfies the Reading Literature CCSS identified for this lesson, it does not extend into supporting students' ELA disciplinary literacy knowledge. However, reading familiar fairytales that vary by cultural perspective may both engage students and extend literacy learning.

In this case, extending the fairytale focus might involve considering emphasis on reinterpretation in different cultures, with a minor focus on the original text, to increase students' access to sophisticated patterns and unexpected elements of text. As this lesson highlights, there are a number of retellings of *Little Red Riding Hood* that draw on elements of that fairytale to transform the story into entirely new cultural settings and genres. In our process of text selection, we first determined that a traditional form of the fairytale, using a leveled text, might be required by schools. Specifically, we suggest a leveled PDF version available through the Reading A–Z website (www.readinga-z.com/book.php?id=2533). We suggest students first read this leveled text of the traditional *Little Red Riding Hood* fairytale to familiarize themselves with the story and plot. Then, other multicultural versions of the text might be introduced and used to build on that reading.

For example, a distinctive element of text selection for this lesson is to select multimodal texts that can support students in purposeful reading and understanding of texts that may be too difficult for independent reading, while also providing opportunities to gain skills needed to critique and analyze digital texts. The text *Petite Rouge: A Cajun Red Riding Hood* (Artell, 2001) is written as a rhyming story and utilizes a Cajun dialect and vocabulary in concert with changes in the characters, setting, and a number of plot points to immerse readers in Cajun culture. However, because many of the words are spelled phonetically, it can be a challenging book for many readers at the 2nd-grade level. Thus, a multimodal book with images, text, and dialectically appropriate audio would support students in reading this text.

Because students will be focusing on a compare and contrast standard, and the primary focus will not be on *Little Red Riding Hood*, the text *Lon Po Po: A Red-Riding Hood Story from China* (Young, 2016) also is selected. With human characters and imagery rooted in a Chinese landscape, this illustrated traditional text can support students' analysis of an additional culture. We want to highlight that *Lon Po Po* is a 4th-grade-level text. But, this selection of a higher-level text was purposeful, as we wanted to include a range of texts for students to consider and compare/contrast, and we aimed to vary the methods in which students consumed these texts. We include it here as a teacher read-aloud to the whole class, but it also could be included as an individual activity supported by a read-aloud digital tool, such as Audible.

Phase 4: Assessing Disciplinary Literacy with a Variety of Tools

Responses to text in the discipline of English use a wide variety of tools and formats to indicate knowledge of literature, composition, linguistics, and vocabulary. In this lesson, the learning objectives and Core Disciplinary Practice indicate that students will need opportunities to provide evidence of learning related to *analyzing text*, including recognizing and analyzing patterns, understanding and examining stories for unexpected elements, and demonstrating fluency, as demonstrated in Table 4.1.

Existing assessments for this lesson might include a Venn diagram handout and fluency passages from a core curriculum or class basal reader. While a Venn diagram handout is a useful tool for compare and contrast learning, there are a number of constraints, such as finite space for writing, need for appropriate writing skills, and identical structure for all students, which may not support all learners.

Using a digital version of a Venn diagram, such as the 2nd-grade-friendly version at readwritethink.org, would allow students increased opportunities to design their own diagram and support the development of ELA disciplinary literacy. This version allows students with a variety of skills to communicate their learning. Students can add circles to their diagram; use brief titles or elaborate with longer explanations; use color and size to communicate different texts, ideas, or importance; and draw on direct quotes from the text or use single-word phrases, among others. Further, because of the enhanced space options, students can integrate their analysis of patterns with the unexpected elements for a single cohesive assessment. These diagrams then can be saved or shared digitally, so that students can share their analyses with another class or beyond the classroom.

To support fluency assessment, students could focus primarily on the leveled text related to *Little Red Riding Hood* and conduct repeated readings. These repeated readings would be recorded to create an audio file, and students would select one of the repeated readings to post along with their Venn diagram that focuses on comparing and contrasting versions of *Little Red Riding Hood*. Along with the selected recording, students can record themselves responding orally to the two essential questions and explaining their analysis from their Venn diagram. The result of the digital Venn diagram, selected repeated reading, and oral response to the two essential questions is a digital performance assessment that demonstrates students' robust understanding of the learning objectives for this lesson. We also recommend using a checklist or rubric, or combination, to focus and guide assessment. A sample checklist-style rubric for this lesson is provided in Figure 4.2.

Phase 5: Digitally Supporting Disciplinary Literacy Instruction

In this lesson, it is critical that all students have a functional knowledge of the plot and characters of *Little Red Riding Hood*. Thus, a leveled version

Figure 4.2. Sample Checklist Rubric

Focal Skills for *Little Red Riding Hood*:

1. Student can read a leveled section of *Little Red Riding Hood* with:

__ Appropriate speed

__ Accuracy

__ Prosody (proper expression)

Notes:

2. Student's ability to draw comparisons between texts:

__ Developing

__ Proficient

__ Exemplary

Notes:

3. Student's ability to contrast texts:

__ Developing

__ Proficient

__ Exemplary

Notes:

4. Student was able to examine/explain unexpected story elements in:

__ *Lon Po Po*

__ *Petite Rouge*

__ Leveled *Little Red Riding Hood*

Notes:

that represents the classic characters, setting, and plot, but on a reading level specific to different reading abilities, may be useful. Because the analysis in this lesson is focused on multiple variations of *Little Red Riding Hood*, using a leveled text in the beginning of the lesson serves to provide the necessary plot, setting, and character information needed to engage in the analysis of the other texts. The leveled version represented in this lesson has the full text with illustrations, which can be used to support a variety of learners. Recognizing the key elements within *Little Red Riding Hood* is important to the more sophisticated analysis that happens later in the lesson and as part of the performance assessment.

Also, key to this lesson is understanding the basic, common elements of fairytales as a fundamental pattern across all three texts. Thus, planning instruction that builds on the knowledge gained from listening to *Little Red Riding Hood*, and building a basic plot diagram to specifically identify what parts may be present in other fairytales, will be useful to prepare students to understand and comprehend *Petite Rouge* and *Lon Po Po*. Again, the

Figure 4.3. Example of Storyboard Created Using Storyboard That for *Petite Rouge*

digital format of the plot diagram allows for collaboration and sharing with the teacher and other students, and provides students a platform to use different modalities, beyond writing, to express their understanding. Students also can utilize a digital tool such as Storyboard That (www.storyboardthat. com) with the two retellings to support their own understanding. This digital tool allows students to save and revise and share in a number of different formats where a teacher could provide feedback or support (see Figure 4.3 for an example).

We close discussion of this phase by specifically pointing out that in this example we integrated digital tools throughout the ELA lesson to support students' learning. However, sometimes only a singular digital tool, used in one part of a lesson, is necessary or useful. Much of this decision lies in teachers' comfort with and knowledge of using digital tools, and we illustrate this varied use of digital tools in subsequent lesson plans in this book.

Phase 6: Reflecting to Reach All Learners

As we discussed in Chapter 2, we recognize that this phase is highly contextual to individual teachers and their students. There are a number of strengths of this lesson related to the specific points of reflection in the PEDDL Framework, including multiple options to show learning, student-directed decisions and options for completing tasks, digital tools that can be used to differentiate instruction for students with different skill levels and to support students with disabilities, and culturally responsive texts. To make this lesson as widely relevant as possible, we invite readers to imagine the ways in which you would use Phase 6 in your own planning of this or a similar ELA lesson.

QUESTIONS TO PONDER

1. What are the advantages of a digital storyboard over a traditional storyboard that students can complete on paper?

We like the digital storyboard format, particularly in the elementary grades, because it supports a variety of modalities in representing understanding and analysis of text. For example, students who do not have advanced writing skills may be able to illustrate their understandings more appropriately and accurately using images and voice-over. These oral explanations might help teachers to gauge students' analysis more accurately.

2. How do digital recordings of retellings better support students' fluency practice?

To us, the purpose of the digital recordings is to allow students more opportunities for practice and focused feedback on fluency from teachers, since teachers do not have to sit down one-on-one with each student to evaluate this skill. As we will note in a subsequent chapter, teachers can quickly record feedback using a digital recorder app and share it with students and parents, cutting down on the time it takes to assess fluency.

3. I'm having a hard time keeping up with the different digital resources I find. How can I better organize those resources?

We like to use digital bookmarking and annotation tools, such as Diigo (www.diigo.com), to bookmark websites and resources we find useful and annotate how we used them for future reference. The great thing about many of these sites is that they are social, and teachers can share their annotated bookmarked sites with one another to create a large repository of digital tools specific to different disciplines.

Hopefully, some of these questions and questions raised in future "Practical Approaches" chapters will be useful to teachers as they plan. As Hutchison and Woodward (2014b) addressed, it is important to consider potential obstacles or critical considerations when integrating digital tools into literacy instruction, and we believe this advice is also relevant for disciplinary literacy instruction. We hope that teachers will take a few moments to consider these questions here and in other "Practical Approaches" chapters and their relevance to the teachers' own classrooms. If obstacles or barriers outweigh the advantages of integrating digital tools, we encourage teachers to reconsider the tool and look for a different tool or a nondigital tool to support disciplinary literacy instruction. For further consideration of planning digitally supported disciplinary literacy in ELA, we provide a 5th-grade lesson plan in online Appendix A using the PEDDL Lesson Plan Template. In it, we continue to focus on *analyzing text* and shift to an emphasis on voice in literature and how immigrant experiences may be presented from a literary standpoint.

Examining Disciplinary Literacy in Elementary Mathematics

Ms. Branch's mathematics instruction is focused primarily on the district curriculum that provides a scope and sequence, materials, and instruction related to the Common Core State Standards. Ms. Branch wants to reframe her existing instruction in math, but also is hesitant to change much about the existing curriculum, as she lacks experience with disciplinary literacy in math. While she understands the important role that mathematical thinking plays in math instruction, she continues to seek new ways to incorporate this into her instruction and rely less on memorization and repeated practice. She begins by targeting the standard:

> CCSS.Math.Content.3.MD.B.3. Draw a scaled picture graph and a scaled bar graph to represent a data set with several categories.

As she is reflecting on her existing instruction, she recognizes that many of the materials and examples she has relied on in class to represent the types of data in this standard do not reflect the diversity of the students in her class. Thus, she is keenly focused on designing math instruction that welcomes students into mathematical thinking through connections to their own and others' lived experiences.

INTEGRATING DISCIPLINARY LITERACY INTO MATHEMATICS

As we turn to disciplinary literacy in mathematics, we do so with the understanding that literacy instruction in math, even from a disciplinary perspective, is less prevalent than literacy instruction in other content areas. However, improving disciplinary literacy in such content areas as mathematics has become such a priority in U.S. education that the national Common Core State Standards (NGACBP & CCSS, 2010) have made recommendations for literacy-based instruction in every core content area (i.e., English, math, science, and social studies) taught in U.S. public schools. In mathematics, students are expected to construct knowledge by reading, analyzing, and writing mathematical text (e.g., numbers, symbols, graphs) in a manner similar to a disciplinary expert, or mathematician (Siebert & Draper, 2012). Although mathematical expertise ranges widely from theoretical to applied mathematics, for purposes of elementary instruction, we consider disciplinary literacy in mathematics to focus on comprehension and application of mathematics. Therefore, our discussion of mathematical disciplinary literacy instruction in this chapter, and the lesson-planning approach detailed in Chapter 6, are centered on application-focused problem solving to determine expert-focused approaches applicable to the real world (De Lange, 2003).

Who Are Mathematics Experts and What Do They Practice?

From a disciplinary perspective, students are expected to construct knowledge by reading, analyzing, and writing mathematical text in a manner similar to an expert (Siebert & Draper, 2012). However, various fields of expertise are grounded in mathematics. Therefore, we keep in mind that mathematical experts may not always be mathematicians. Consider engineers—mathematics is often at the heart of their work, for example, in designing machinery, supporting building and bridge structures, and developing efficient methods of transportation for organic and chemical products. Accountants and financial planners also use and apply mathematics rigorously in their work to run companies' and individuals' budgets efficiently, and would be considered experts. Have you ever bought or sold a house? If so, you have firsthand experience of the mathematics expertise required in real estate. We note these varying fields to illustrate the many different ways mathematics instruction can be disciplinary.

Specifically, the National Council of Teachers of Mathematics (2013) outlines multiple practices that align with expertise in mathematics:

- Problem solving
- Engaging in reasoning and proof
- Communication of mathematical ideas
- Drawing connections between mathematical ideas
- Developing representations of mathematical ideas

These practices suggest a high level of application in mathematical expertise. These practices also indicate a process in disciplinary literacy in math that requires students to actively read, comprehend, and engage with problems, both numerical and word-based, to develop solutions and communicate those solutions. Students should be able to communicate to real audiences, either in writing or orally, their solutions using mathematical language. Table 5.1 breaks down these practices and connects them to the Core Disciplinary Practices that structure our approach to disciplinary literacy in elementary grades.

Table 5.1. Connections Between Expert and Core Mathematics Practices

Mathematics Expert Practices	Core Disciplinary Practices
• Problem solving • Drawing connections between mathematical ideas	• Recognizing or comprehending multiple types of text • Analysis across multiple texts
• Communication of mathematical ideas	• Comprehending and using vocabulary particular to a discipline
• Engaging in reasoning and proof • Developing representations of mathematical ideas	• Developing and communicating ideas, arguments, or rationalizations

Similar to when we connected core ELA practices to expert practices in Chapter 3, some of these look quite different at the elementary-grade level than how they are enacted by experts, or even in middle and high school. For example, it is not until middle school, at the earliest, that using formulas and conceptual mathematical processes to undergird an understanding of the connections between mathematical ideas and to engage in reasoning and proofs is introduced in mathematics curricula. However, elementary students often are able to engage in this type of thinking through understanding similarities between mathematical functions and generating rationales for multiple types of problem solving. Thus, in this chapter, we focus primarily on problem solving, communication of mathematical ideas, and developing representations of mathematical ideas to serve as a foundation for developing disciplinary literacy in mathematics.

What Role Do Digital Tools Play in Expert Mathematics Practices?

When thinking about digitally supported disciplinary literacy, it can be useful to look at the digital tools commonly used by math experts in the field. Although too advanced for elementary integration, many of these tools can prompt consideration of technological features (e.g., organization, graphic representation) important to the study of mathematics. Table 5.2 outlines some of these tools by area of expertise, with connections to the types of tools that might be supportive of disciplinary literacy in mathematical learning.

This list is not comprehensive. However, it provides a glimpse at the features of digital mathematics tools, used by experts, that may be relevant to K–5 learning. At the very least, we hope that discussing with students how experts use digital (and other supporting) tools will prompt connections to the use of mathematics in the real world, since it is important for students to form out-of-school disciplinary connections with math learning.

Table 5.2. Expert Digital Tool Connections

Expert	Professional Digital Tools	Possibilities for Classroom Application
Mathematician	• Graphing calculator • Digital modeling simulator • Spreadsheet software • Mathematical computing software for analysis and simulation • Mathematical language software to interpret/develop symbols-based language	• Digital representations of mathematical ideas or solutions • Graphic organizers of mathematical concepts • Exploring different solutions to problems
Engineer	• Drafting software • Flow meters (measure flow rates of liquids and gases) • Process simulation software	• Digital representations of mathematical ideas or solutions • Digital measurements
Accountant/ Financial Planner	• Calculator • Spreadsheet software • Payroll software • Book-keeping software • Tax software	• Digital and/or graphic organization of numerical data • Opportunities to work with data

What Standards Promote Disciplinary Literacy in Mathematics?

We again turn to the CCSS to draw deliberate connections between standards and the Core Disciplinary Practices outlined in this book. Chapter 6 also will focus on these connections in the sample lesson plan based on the PEDDL Framework. In mathematics, the CCSS focus heavily on conceptual understandings and mathematical principles that build and progress with each grade level. Particularly, "the knowledge and skills students need to be prepared for mathematics in college, career, and life are woven throughout the mathematics standards" (Common Core State Standards Initiative, 2019). We highlight this statement as a direct connection to disciplinary learning that targets math skills that support students in careers and in life beginning in kindergarten. To illustrate connections between math standards and Core Disciplinary Practices, in Table 5.3 we highlight standards and action-based language in each grade to draw attention to the different ways disciplinary literacy skills might be incorporated in K–5 classrooms.

Table 5.3. Math Standards and Disciplinary Literacy Practices

Grade Level	Mathematics CCSS
K	CCSS.Math.Content.K.OA.A.1 Represent addition and subtraction with objects, fingers, mental images, drawings, sounds (e.g., claps), acting out situations, verbal explanations, expressions, or equations. CCSS.Math.Content.K.G.B.4 Analyze and compare two- and three-dimensional shapes, in different sizes and orientations, using informal language to describe their similarities, differences, parts (e.g., number of sides and vertices/"corners") and other attributes (e.g., having sides of equal length).
1	CCSS.Math.Content.1.NBT.B.3 Compare two two-digit numbers based on meanings of the tens and ones digits, recording the results of comparisons with the symbols >, =, and <. CCSS.Math.Content.1.MD.C.4 Organize, represent, and interpret data with up to three categories; ask and answer questions about the total number of data points, how many in each category, and how many more or less are in one category than in another.
2	CCSS.Math.Content.2.NBT.B.7 Add and subtract within 1000, using concrete models or drawings and strategies based on place value, properties of operations, and/or the relationship between addition and subtraction; relate the strategy to a written method. Understand that in adding or subtracting three-digit numbers, one adds or subtracts hundreds and hundreds, tens and tens, ones and ones; and sometimes it is necessary to compose or decompose tens or hundreds. CCSS.Math.Content.2.G.A.1 Recognize and draw shapes having specified attributes, such as a given number of angles or a given number of equal faces. Identify triangles, quadrilaterals, pentagons, hexagons, and cubes.

Although real-world application language is not used specifically until 5th grade, the standards promote grade-appropriate disciplinary practices that build up to students being able to independently use and apply mathematics in real-world settings. Indeed, the standards were developed to promote disciplinary mathematical practices throughout K–5 instruction. For instance, the Common Core State Standards Initiative (2019) describes the following practices, which are identical across elementary grades:

Table 5.3. Math Standards and Disciplinary Literacy Practices *(continued)*

Grade Level	Mathematics CCSS
3	CCSS.Math.Content.3.NF.A.3 Explain equivalence of fractions in special cases, and compare fractions by reasoning about their size. CCSS.Math.Content.3.MD.B.3 Draw a scaled picture graph and a scaled bar graph to represent a data set with several categories. Solve one- and two-step "how many more" and "how many less" problems using information presented in scaled bar graphs.
4	CCSS.Math.Content.4.OA.A.3 Solve multistep word problems posed with whole numbers and having whole-number answers using the four operations, including problems in which remainders must be interpreted. Represent these problems using equations with a letter standing for the unknown quantity. Assess the reasonableness of answers using mental computation and estimation strategies including rounding. CCSS.Math.Content.4.NBT.B.5 Multiply a whole number of up to four digits by a one-digit whole number, and multiply two two-digit numbers, using strategies based on place value and the properties of operations. Illustrate and explain the calculation by using equations, rectangular arrays, and/or area models.
5	CCSS.Math.Content.5.MD.A.1 Convert among different-sized standard measurement units within a given measurement system (e.g., convert 5 cm to 0.05 m), and use these conversions in solving multi-step, real-world problems. CCSS.Math.Content.5.G.A.2 Represent real-world and mathematical problems by graphing points in the first quadrant of the coordinate plane, and interpret coordinate values of points in the context of the situation.

- Make sense of problems and persevere in solving them.
- Reason abstractly and quantitatively.
- Construct viable arguments and critique the reasoning of others.
- Model with mathematics.
- Use appropriate tools strategically.
- Attend to precision.
- Look for and make use of structure.
- Look for and express regularity in related reasoning.

We draw attention to these practices and to the discrepancies between levels of disciplinary focus in K–5 standards to note that disciplinary connections might not be as clear in earlier grades, but the skills promoted are required for basic or future disciplinary literacy learning. This is particularly important to remember in elementary grades, where disciplinary literacy often looks different than in higher grades.

Selecting Texts for Disciplinary Literacy in Mathematics

We continually discuss in this book our perspective, and a consistent theme in disciplinary literacy, that texts are any resources that can be read, analyzed, or produced. Mathematics, unlike ELA, focuses primarily on texts that are not word-based. Text in mathematics may be number- or symbol-based and requires a reconsideration of reading and comprehension skills. We note that it is common to see word problems as a primary focus when discussing literacy in mathematics. Although word problems can be a part of disciplinary literacy instruction in mathematics, a disciplinary lens considers graphs, tables, numbers, formulas, or symbols also to be relevant mathematical texts.

Increasingly, these texts are created and shared utilizing digital tools. Disciplinary experts rely heavily on digital tools to manage data, explore different outcomes of problems, model solutions, and present information. Students may use numbers in a textbook or in another traditional print text to inform the creation of a digital graph or table. Further, mathematical texts often are combined with figures or other types of texts to create multimodal texts with a variety of features.

Table 5.4 continues to expand Colwell's (2019) Disciplinary Text Selection Table to include a variety of print, digital, and multimodal mathematics texts useful for disciplinary literacy instruction.

Again, we emphasize cultural and social relevance in text selection, as the texts students are presented with, or create, serve as powerful tools in providing engaging instruction and reaching all learners. Particularly in mathematics, we encourage teachers to think about text creation as the result of solving or addressing a problem that is culturally or socially relevant, and we propose allowing students to create a variety of text types that suit their particular learning needs. For example, producing a line graph on traditional graph paper may be difficult for students with visual or motor disabilities, or students who are still developing fine motor skills. Using a digital graphing tool, where the sizes can be manipulated and the level of control required to create the graph is lessened, can allow students to create a digitally supported disciplinary text that fits their learning needs. In addressing real-world issues, students can learn about the importance of mathematics in out-of-school settings. For example, students can identify how many vegetables are produced from their school garden, ask the health

Table 5.4. Modified Disciplinary Literacy Text Selection for Mathematics

Print, Digital, and Other Multimodal Text Types	Questions to Consider
Symbols Shapes (3-D digital and nondigital) Proofs Equations Graphs (digital and nondigital) Charts (digital and nondigital) Formulas	• Does the text I selected represent an idea or problem grounded in mathematics that can connect to students' lives? • Is the text available in multiple formats (print, digital, multimodal) to support all learners? • Can the text be used to solve or illustrate a socially or culturally relevant issue or problem in mathematics? • Can the text be used to support learners who may struggle with mathematics? • What additional text(s) might support the same mathematical idea or problem to provide additional perspectives on approaches or solutions? • What texts (digital and nondigital) will students create to support mathematical literacy?

and nutrition director how that food is used as part of the school lunch program, and calculate the impact that their school garden has on feeding students in their school.

HOW CAN DISCIPLINARY LITERACY INSTRUCTION BE DIGITALLY SUPPORTED IN MATHEMATICS?

Proponents of digital tools to support disciplinary instruction argue that thoughtful integration can provide increased opportunities for collaboration, creative production, and creative problem solving, leading to new ways to explore and explain disciplinary concepts (Castek & Manderino, 2017). To achieve these potential instructional engagements and improvements, digital tools must be integrated thoughtfully and with a focus on the instructional goals they are intended to support (Colwell & Hutchison, 2015). Keeping this in mind, we turn to the four Core Disciplinary Practices for disciplinary literacy in elementary grades and how digital tools and literacy strategies might be incorporated to support each in mathematics.

Recognizing and Comprehending Multiple Types of Mathematics Texts

It is important, first and foremost in disciplinary literacy in math, for elementary students to gain familiarity with texts that are considered mathematical.

These texts will look different from the more traditional associations they might have with the word text in, for example, English language arts. Table 5.5 proposes sample literacy strategies and digital tools that can support recognition and subsequent comprehension of different math texts. As we did in Chapter 3 when providing strategies and digital tool examples for the Core Disciplinary Practices in ELA, we use a common theme here (i.e., plane shapes) and show how it may be built upon as we move into higher elementary-grade levels.

Table 5.5. Literacy Strategies to Support Recognition and Comprehension of Multiple Types of Mathematics Texts

Grade Level	Literacy Strategy	Digital Tool	Example
1st	Open shape sort (modified word sort)	Digital table and voice recorder	Students digitally drag and drop geometric plane shape images into categories in a digital table provided by the teacher and explain their categories so the teacher can assess prior knowledge.
3rd	Annotation	Graphic organizer on a computer or tablet	Students place a polygon (e.g., a hexagon) at the center of a digital graphic organizer and then digitally partition the polygon into equal areas. Then students annotate, using text bubbles, each part as a fraction of a whole and describe the resulting shape using geometric terms. This activity could be done multiple times for practice, as students can wipe clean their annotated polygon after taking a screenshot for teacher assessment.
5th	Modeling comprehension	Interactive whiteboard on class-connected tablets (i.e., Nearpod)	The teacher models using perpendicular lines to create a coordinate system with axes and coordinates on the interactive whiteboard, which displays on each student's tablet. Students then practice representing different units in the coordinate system and share their attempts with the teacher's tablet as well as with other students in the class for immediate feedback.

Analyzing Mathematics Texts

We have found that elementary teachers are somewhat wary of considering analysis in mathematics. This is not to say that they do not agree that students should analyze mathematical texts. Instead, teachers often wonder *how* they can support students in math text analysis and what that even looks like in instruction. From a disciplinary literacy perspective, the analysis of mathematical texts typically manifests as a part of problem solving, regardless of whether word-based text is present. Students should analyze texts to rationalize an answer or a response to a problem, formula, or graph/chart-focused representation of data.

We discussed in Chapter 3 how close reading has become an integral part of ELA analysis in elementary grades. Indeed, word-based texts play a large role in students' early learning and exposure to texts. These types of texts absolutely play a role in math as students can develop mathematical representations of a word-based problem. Yet, at the elementary level, where students are beginning to consider numbers, graphs, charts, and shapes as texts that can be read and analyzed, it also can be useful to draw appropriate connections between analysis in ELA and in mathematics to support student learning. As Halladay and Neumann (2012) suggest, using analysis-focused language in both ELA and math is beneficial to prompt student analysis. For example, teachers might ask students to make predictions; use self-monitoring behaviors to confirm comprehension; locate important information; and draw connections between texts and life (Halladay & Neumann, 2012). Table 5.6 discusses explicit strategies and digital tools that support students in analysis of mathematics texts.

Using Vocabulary Particular to Mathematics

A key element of disciplinary literacy in mathematics is being able to accurately use and understand math-related vocabulary. Precision is necessary to accurately describe mathematical procedures and processes. Additionally, conceptual understandings in math are strongly related to the appropriate use of mathematical terminology (Caparo, Caparo, & Rupley, 2010). Although much focus has been directed at adolescents and mathematical vocabulary learning, it is important to consider the role of vocabulary in elementary mathematics to lay a foundation for student recognition and use of math-related vocabulary.

The vocabulary demands of mathematics vary widely from units of measurements to specific operations, from methods of modeling and presenting mathematical data to ratios and relationships. The Mathematics CCSS provide a useful Mathematics Glossary that organizes important terms into tables with relevant examples in a problem context. Tables 1 and 2 of that

Table 5.6. Literacy Strategies to Support Analysis of Mathematics Texts

Grade Level	Literacy Strategy	Digital Tool	Example
K	Read-write-pair-share	Audio-supported annotation tool (e.g., Educreations)	Students individually study a pie chart representing a tally of students' favorite seasons. They audio-record their interpretation of the chart, swap audio recordings with a partner, and talk about similarities and differences of interpretations.
2	Split-page note-taking	Shareable table on tablets or laptops	The class studies an image of a produce section in a grocery store the teacher has copied into the left side of a digital table shared on all students' devices. The class locates a group of produce that is an even number. Students take turns digitally circling pairs in that group to represent the total number. In the right-hand column students collaboratively type/write an equation to express the even number as a sum of two equal addends.
4	Summarizing	Internet news resource	Students will locate a news article on Newsela that provides numerical data on a current problem of interest (global warming, pollution, etc.). Students then will compile and summarize the information using a graphing tool (digital or print-based) to illustrate the problem mathematically.

document are most relevant to elementary learners and include terms related to addition (e.g., add to, more), subtraction (e.g., take from, fewer), multiplication (e.g., equal groups, area), division (e.g., dividend, quotient), and measurement (e.g., centimeters, inches). Table 5.7 identifies specific examples of how to support students' disciplinary knowledge of mathematical vocabulary.

Communicating in Mathematics

Directly related to vocabulary in mathematics, it is important for students to be able to communicate mathematical problems, ideas, claims, and

Table 5.7. Literacy Strategies to Support Mathematics Vocabulary Instruction

Grade Level	Literacy Strategy	Digital Tool	Example
1	Text impressions	Digital drawing application	The teacher will give students 3–4 mathematical terms that relate to analyzing chart data and then ask students to doodle their impressions of the terms and digitally share and explain their doodles to the class or a small group.
3	Frayer Model or vocabulary card	Digital graphic organizer	Students will use an application or website to create a four-square vocabulary card on the term *equivalence* in regard to fractions. The model will provide the word, definition, illustration, and nonexample or contrasting example.
5	Word wall	Collaborative class website	As a class, students and the teacher will develop a digital word wall focused specifically on mathematical vocabulary terms important to engaging in mathematical processes. This wall may contain words or symbols. Students and the teacher can access the word wall in and outside of the classroom, and the word wall is editable. However, if a word or symbol has been added/edited, the teacher will review with the class to ensure accurate representation.

responses or solutions. This communication should take various forms, including but not limited to writing claims using mathematically appropriate text; orally explaining mathematical understandings; discussing mathematical problems with the teacher, classmates, and other relevant audiences; and rationalizing mathematical solutions.

Digitally supported disciplinary literacy instruction in mathematics extends these communication forms through examining the particular contributions that digital tools can make to student learning. Table 5.8 provides examples of different approaches to communication within mathematics and literacy strategies and digital tools that support those approaches.

Table 5.8. Literacy Strategies to Communicate in Mathematics

Grade Level	Literacy Strategy	Digital Tool	Example
1	Think-aloud	Tablet speech-to-text tool or audio recording	A learning station will provide students with individual access to a tablet that has speech-to-text capabilities or a recording feature. Students will read a word problem focused on adding three whole numbers and orally explain their approach to addition and how they arrived at their answer, using mathematically correct terms.
3	Response writing	Screencast	Students will find or be provided with three digital images of analog clocks set at different times. They will create a screencast where they discuss and tell the time on each clock to the nearest minute.
5	Collaborative conversations	Video slideshow maker	In partners, students will discuss their interpretation of dividing a whole number by a fraction and create a video slideshow of a story context showing where and how that division process would be used (e.g., baking a cake that is ¼ the size of the standard recipe).

Practical Approaches to Digitally Supported Disciplinary Literacy in Mathematics

In this chapter, we will focus on the Core Disciplinary Practice of *developing and communicating ideas, arguments, or rationalizations*. Although, on the surface, it may not seem that this core practice is closely related to mathematics, there are multiple reasons for even early elementary students to learn it. We present our thinking on this topic through a kindergarten lesson on representing and explaining addition. In this lesson we provide a thorough analysis of how we used the PEDDL Framework to develop a disciplinary mathematics lesson that would be appropriate for kindergarten. As in our ELA "Practical Approaches" chapter, we provide an additional mathematics lesson focused on this topic in another grade level in online Appendix B to highlight the use of the PEDDL Lesson Plan Template.

SAMPLE LESSON:
REPRESENTING AND EXPLAINING ADDITION IN KINDERGARTEN

In this sample lesson, we focus on the core practice of *communicating ideas, arguments, and rationalizations*, as this is an important practice but often not the primary focus in elementary mathematics. Nevertheless, communication and rationalizations have become key areas of focus in national and many states' mathematics standards. This lesson particularly uses the CCSS to highlight the integration of this core practice into kindergarten instruction.

Phase 1: Identifying Appropriate Disciplinary Literacy Practices

To consider how to integrate disciplinary literacy practices into mathematics, we again begin with Phase 1 of the PEDDL Framework (see Table 6.1). We start with a common kindergarten mathematics national standard focused on representing addition and subtraction: Represent addition and subtraction with objects, fingers, mental images, drawings, sounds (e.g., claps), acting out situations, verbal explanations, expressions, or equations (CCSS Math.Content.K.OA.A.1). Upon examining this standard, we see that there are clear connections to the core disciplinary literacy practices discussed in prior chapters. For example, this standard suggests that students should represent their ideas and provide explanations. Accordingly, this standard closely relates to the Core Disciplinary Practices of (a) *Comprehending and Using Vocabulary Particular to a Discipline* and (b) *Communicating Ideas, Arguments, or Rationalizations.*

By focusing on *Communicating Ideas, Arguments, or Rationalizations,* we can reinforce the importance of explaining one's thinking and the ability to create representations of mathematical ideas. We particularly focus on this Core Disciplinary Practice in kindergarten, as mathematics instruction, in recent years, has taken a much sharper turn, across K–12 instruction, toward students being able to show *how* they arrived at a mathematical conclusion, rather than simply providing an end product to be evaluated as correct or incorrect.

As the lesson objectives in Table 6.1 highlight, we focus in this lesson only on addition, and the original lesson objective is for students to create an addition sentence using illustrations. Figure 6.1 shows an example of a traditional worksheet problem teachers might use to teach this standard.

As the worksheet illustrates, students would first count objects to fill in the blank and then use the model to draw their own number. Although this approach does allow students to represent addition as mentioned in the standard, it provides only one way for students to represent addition. Furthermore, this approach does not encourage students to use disciplinary vocabulary or explain their thinking. Thus, revising the lesson to include

Figure 6.1. Example of Typical Approach for Teaching the Standard

Table 6.1. Planning Outline

Current Instructional Considerations	Disciplinary Extensions
PHASE 1: Identifying Appropriate Disciplinary Literacy Practices	
What state/national standards am I targeting? CCSS.Math.Content.K.OA.A.1. Represent addition and subtraction with objects, fingers, mental images, drawings, sounds (e.g., claps), acting out situations, verbal explanations, expressions, or equations. **What are my lesson objectives?** *Original objective:* Students will create an addition sentence using illustrations. *Revised objectives after adding disciplinary extensions:* 1. Students will create 1–3 addition number sentences and represent their ideas through illustrations, objects, sounds, or acting. 2. Students will orally explain their addition number sentence and representation using appropriate mathematics vocabulary (e.g., plus, equals, fact, addend, sum).	**What Core Disciplinary Practice is supported by those standards and objectives?** Developing and communicating ideas, arguments, or rationalizations
PHASE 2: Framing Disciplinary Literacy	
What information is important for my students to learn and understand from this lesson? How to represent and explain their understanding of addition	**Why is it important for students to learn and understand this topic?** In most jobs involving mathematics, professionals must explain their reasoning for arriving at a particular sum or solution. Professionals must be able to represent complex mathematical solutions in a way that is easily understandable by nonexperts. Although kindergarten students are not ready for this level of complexity, we can begin to prepare them by posing the following essential question (EQ): 1. What is the connection of addition to (a) other mathematics knowledge, ideas, or symbols we have learned; (b) yourself or your home; (c) your community or the world?

(table continues on next page)

Table 6.1. Planning Outline *(continued)*

Current Instructional Considerations	Disciplinary Extensions
PHASE 3: Selecting Multimodal Texts for Disciplinary Literacy	
What texts does my school or school district require when teaching this topic? Manipulatives, math workbook What texts do I feel comfortable using to support students' learning? Which topical texts align with my students' current reading levels? The picture book *Mission: Addition* by Loreen Leedy (1997), presented as a read-aloud since students would not be able to read this independently	What digital and multimodal texts might supplement my currently used texts and extend students' learning to encourage disciplinary literacy? Animated videos that illustrate and explain addition concepts How might these digital and multimodal texts help support students to engage in more advanced reading, writing, and communication practices? Animated videos would provide a model of the kind of illustration and explanation that students are expected to do.
PHASE 4: Assessing Disciplinary Literacy with a Variety of Tools	
What assessments do I currently use to determine students' learning and understanding of this topic? Worksheets What type(s) of knowledge (e.g., fact-based, process-based, etc.) do those assessments gauge? Fact-based/right or wrong answers	How can I incorporate digital tools to further assess students' understanding of disciplinary practices and texts? Use of a digital tool that will enable students to create illustrations, show objects, or act out an addition sentence and record oral explanations. Recording oral explanations is important since many kindergarten students cannot yet write explanations. How do these digital tools create or support a more comprehensive assessment of students' understanding? They provide the teacher with an original addition sentence created by students and give students many choices for representing addition. The oral explanation gives students the opportunity to appropriately use disciplinary vocabulary and enables teachers to determine whether and when misconceptions occur, whether vocabulary is used correctly, and what kind of support or clarification is needed.

Table 6.1. Planning Outline (*continued*)

Current Instructional Considerations	Disciplinary Extensions
PHASE 5: Digitally Supporting Disciplinary Literacy Instruction	
How do I prepare my students to learn this topic? Read a book on addition to activate their prior knowledge. **How do I guide my students' comprehension of this topic?** Represent content in multiple ways. **How do I help my students reflect on their learning of this topic?** Students listen to recordings of their oral explanations to determine accuracy and completion.	
PHASE 6: Reflecting to Reach All Learners	
How have I differentiated instruction in this lesson? Students choose what kind of number sentence they create; videos and images will build background knowledge and present content in different formats.	**How have I considered personal, social, and cultural understandings that inform this lesson?** Through the essential question guiding the lesson students are encouraged to make connections from math to themselves and the world. Students can add their responses to the essential question to their audio recording as an opportunity for further reflection.

one or more of the Core Disciplinary Practices enables the teacher to take advantage of the time spent on this standard to also provide opportunities for speaking and listening. As can be seen in Table 6.1, adding a disciplinary literacy focus to the lesson also requires that the original lesson objectives be revised. Similarly, the revised objectives will need to be revisited throughout the rest of the planning process with the PEDDL Framework.

Phase 2: Framing Disciplinary Literacy

In Phase 2, we consider how to make this mathematics content relevant to both the real world and the work of experts in this discipline, as well as to the students themselves. It is important first to determine why students need to learn and understand the disciplinary literacy practices related to this topic. In this case, it is important for students to go beyond just learning how to add numbers or objects and how to draw illustrations that represent addition. Indeed, professionals in mathematics fields must be able to explain their mathematical thinking and how they arrived at an answer.

For example, when working with homebuyers, a banker must be able to explain the components of a loan payment and how each part contributes to the whole. Although this explanation is far beyond what is appropriate for kindergarten students, it is important for them to know that mathematics professionals must be able to explain their thinking to nonexperts. We can encourage students to make connections from the content to the world around them by asking an essential question that encourages these connections and makes the content personally relevant. In this case, we have modified the traditional literacy strategy of *making connections* to make it appropriate for math.

Typically, a student would be asked to make connections among text-to-text, text-to-self, and text-to-world. Here we have modified the strategy to ask students to make connections from the mathematics concept of addition to other mathematics knowledge (math-to-math), to themselves (math-to-self), and to the world around them (math-to-world). Encouraging these kinds of connections through the essential question not only enables students to see the relevance of the mathematics concept, but also encourages social relevance. Students are explicitly encouraged to consider how the concept is represented in their own lives and communities.

Phase 3: Selecting Multimodal Texts for Disciplinary Literacy

In Phase 3, we consider what texts, if any, are required for teaching the content, as well as the variety of additional texts that will encourage learning of the Core Disciplinary Practices and support students in engaging in more advanced reading, writing, and communication practices. In many cases, teachers may be required or encouraged to use a particular workbook or set of materials. However, these materials can be supplemented with additional text types, both digital and print, that represent the content in varied and multiple ways.

For this lesson, the first additional text beyond the math workbook is the picture book *Mission: Addition* by Loreen Leedy (1997). This book is particularly appropriate for this lesson for several reasons. First, it contains illustrations of addition number sentences with drawings that represent the number sentences. More important, it explicitly teaches disciplinary vocabulary, introducing the terms *addend, sum, equals,* and *fact.* Further, it is written in sections, making it appropriate for the teacher to read only the part of the book that is most relevant to the lesson. Finally, the content is presented as a mystery and likely to be of high interest to students. Overall, use of this book provides the teacher with a clear opportunity for introducing important mathematics vocabulary that may be useful for students to explicate their thinking and learning.

An additional type of digital text that could support this instruction is animated videos that illustrate and explain the concepts. These videos would be appropriate for all students, but particularly those who need additional exposure to the content. Accordingly, these videos could be assigned as needed as part of mathematics centers. Presenting the content in video form is also useful because videos can provide an additional model of the ways that objects, drawings, sound, and acting can represent addition and how to explain these representations.

Phase 4: Assessing Disciplinary Literacy with a Variety of Tools

Phase 4 of the PEDDL Framework guides us to consider how digital tools can provide unique opportunities for assessment and offer students multiple ways to represent their disciplinary knowledge. Here, we pose that students use a digital tool that enables them to create illustrations, show objects, or act out an addition sentence and record oral explanations. There are many options for this kind of tool, such as a video-recording tool for acting out explanations or an interactive whiteboard tool (e.g., Show Me) for drawing, adding shapes and images, and narrating what is being drawn on the screen.

There are many advantages to using a video-supported digital tool for this assessment. First, by using a digital tool, students have many options for how to represent their work and a way to record their oral explanation. This means that this work could be done during center work and would not require the teacher to listen to each student's oral explanation or presentation during class time. Rather, the teacher could view the saved videos later. Additionally, digitally recording their work gives students the opportunity to self-monitor by listening to their explanation to determine whether it is accurate and complete. Also, a digital work product can be shared easily between school and home to inform parents about class content and allow parents to gain insight into the student's mathematical understanding. This digital work can serve as a starting point for at-home conversations about mathematics. Figure 6.2 shows an example of an addition sentence created with Explain Everything (whiteboard.explaineverything.com). This tool allows students to record their voice and the action on their screen so they can explain their illustrations.

Phase 5: Digitally Supporting Disciplinary Literacy Instruction

In Phase 5 we consider whether there are any digital tools that may help support disciplinary literacy instruction on this topic. We have already added many digital tools to this lesson that are intended to activate students' prior knowledge and support their comprehension. Thus, it is important to

Figure 6.2. Number Sentence and Explanation Created with Explain Everything

recognize that additional digital tools may not always be needed. Rather, teachers just may need to consider how the tools being used can be used in a way to specifically target comprehension of the content. In this case, however, we are adding the use of a Promethean Board to the part of the lesson in which the picture book *Mission: Addition* is being read, to help support and guide comprehension.

Specifically, since picture books require strong oral listening skills, we believe it would be valuable to represent the ideas and vocabulary from the book in additional ways and to have students interact with these ideas and vocabulary to reinforce comprehension. The ideas from the book could be represented again by creating stopping points in which the students could drag and drop objects on the Promethean Board to represent addition sentences from the story. Students also could hear new vocabulary again and locate the symbol or picture that matches the word. Presenting this content with the assistance of a digital tool provides an opportunity for repeated exposure to the content and for representing the content in multiple ways. This may be particularly useful for students who do not have strong listening comprehension and for English learners who may benefit from having the content presented in multiple ways.

Finally, we consider using an audio/video tool to help students record and reflect on their learning through illustration. This type of tool would support synthesis of ideas and development of an artifact to demonstrate understanding. And as students would be using talk and drawing to explain their thinking, this tool would appropriately support kindergarten-level students in disciplinary literacy in math.

Phase 6: Reflecting to Reach All Learners

Phase 6 of the PEDDL Framework encourages us to consider how students' individual interests, backgrounds, and needs are accounted for in the lesson. Specific needs will vary by classroom, but in general we suggest the following guidelines whenever possible: (a) students should have multiple options for representing their ideas, (b) content should be presented in multiple formats, (c) there should be multiple ways for students to get support when needed, (d) students should have options for working alone or collaboratively, and (e) teachers should make content relevant to students' lives and help students discover the personal relevance of the content. Upon reflection, we see that we have followed these guidelines in this lesson.

Specifically, students have multiple options for how they represent addition (objects, illustrations, acting out) and have the opportunity to create an original addition sentence that is of interest to them. The content will be presented in multiple formats with multiple opportunities to revisit the content or hear it in a different way. The multiple formats provide multiple points at which students can get support if they do not understand the content. Although we did not specify earlier, this reflection point helps us to realize that we could provide students with the opportunity to collaborate on the creation of their representations and explanations. Our essential question ensures that we help students see the relevance of the content and be able to connect the content to their own lives.

QUESTIONS TO PONDER

1. **I'm concerned my students will get off task if I make this digital assessment a part of center work. Also, there is only one of me, and I know my students are going to have so many questions in their center work. How can I alleviate these concerns?**

First, our experiences indicate that students who understand the rationale behind the digital work they are engaging in are less likely to veer off task. Make sure students understand exactly what is expected of them, the amount of time they will have to complete the task, and what you are looking for in their end product. This approach creates a more goal-focused center session. We also have found that providing students with concrete directions, and accompanying graphics, helps young elementary students with the questions they might have. Model having a question and referencing the directions at the center before asking a teacher for help. Make the directions explicit and sequential (i.e., First, you should . . . , Second, . . .) so that students can follow the order exactly when they get to the station. We also suggest making this a partner activity with purposeful pairings so that more tech-savvy students can support less tech-savvy students.

2. **The digital component of this assessment seems too intensive when students simply can represent their mathematical understanding using tangible classroom objects (i.e., building blocks). Why should I incorporate digital tools in this context?**

You are correct that there are many ways for students to represent their thinking. However, we highlight here the word *communication* in the Core Disciplinary Practice of focus in this lesson. It is time-consuming for all students to communicate their understanding using real materials and then for the teacher to assess those communications individually during class time. Videos allow students to both visually and verbally explain their thinking, and simultaneously provide foundational digital skills.

We again hope these considerations help teachers to thoughtfully plan instruction that utilizes digital tools in mathematics disciplinary literacy. In online Appendix B, we provide a 3rd-grade lesson plan, using the PEDDL Lesson Plan Template, focused on calculating perimeter to show how digitally supported disciplinary literacy instruction in this context also might support the Core Disciplinary Practice of *Communicating Ideas, Arguments, or Rationalizations*. In it, we highlight the importance of connecting mathematical concepts to out-of-school concepts to underscore the utility of disciplinary mathematics in everyday life.

Examining Disciplinary Literacy in Elementary Science

Ms. Branch is beginning to feel more confident with disciplinary literacy, especially as she looks at her 3rd-grade science curriculum and standards, which align with the recent Next Generation Science Standards. She sees much overlap between disciplinary literacy and her current science instruction. To take advantage of this overlap, she decides to not make further changes to her instruction and instead focus on making the concept of disciplinary literacy in science clear to her students. Also, she aims to better support all learners by incorporating a digital tool that may serve as a scaffold for students to understand and more independently examine scientific concepts. She focuses her instructional planning on inherited traits in animals, as this reflects an existing unit and standards expected in 3rd grade in her school. To do so, she focuses on the Core Disciplinary Practice of *analyzing text* and decides that she can incorporate different types of digital texts, such as videos, interactive simulations, and expert podcasts, as well as traditional texts, to prepare students to engage in their own study of common traits across desert animals.

INTEGRATING DISCIPLINARY LITERACY INTO SCIENCE

Elementary grades offer rich opportunities to begin incorporating disciplinary literacy in science into instruction and exposing students to it. Ms. Branch plans to take advantage of these opportunities to engage her students in digitally supported disciplinary literacy to study inherited traits. Indeed, in science, disciplinary literacy aligns with skills such as hypothesizing, creating research questions, observing, investigating, and making claims based on evidence. These skills are a natural fit for elementary grades, as young children often are naturally inclined to study and inquire about the world around them, and they create prime learning scenarios for investigation in science and studying through a scientific lens (Juel et al., 2010). Juel and colleagues also argued that incorporating disciplinary literacy in science may support students who struggle with comprehension or vocabulary, particularly English language learners, due to the wide range of texts represented and utilized in science. Through a scientific lens, objects, such as rocks; living things, such as plants and animals; and natural phenomena, such as weather, are treated as text that a student can learn to observe and draw conclusions about based on inquiry.

Unlike English and often history, science relies heavily on nonprint-based texts or hybrid texts that use words along with graphics for understanding, and these nontraditional texts promote inquiry and literacy in science (Draper, 2002; Lemke, 2004). In this chapter, we discuss disciplinary literacy instruction in science as a process of studying scientific evidence, and Chapter 8 provides a science lesson that utilizes the PEDDL Framework to put this process into action.

Who Are Science Experts and What Do They Practice?

To be literate in science, students must be able, in the simplest terms, to *do* science (Draper & Adair, 2010). Action through investigation or engagement in scientific activity that promotes discovery lies at the heart of expert practices in science. Scientists, in the broadest terms, systematically conduct research and test collected evidence against a hypothesis to form an evidence-based conclusion. As educators, we regularly see students engaging in investigation, often as early as prekindergarten, making expert practices in science a natural fit for elementary grades.

Science, particularly in the present day, is a wide-reaching field and encompasses many subdisciplines and experts. Scientists may work in a traditional lab in universities, hospitals, and research centers, or they may work in the field under less controlled circumstances. Scientists may be chemists, biologists, geologists, astronomers, zoologists, or physicists. They also may include computer scientists, engineers, or information scientists. Additionally, some scientists work with human subjects and are considered social scientists, such as psychologists and professors who, for example, study education.

As you can see, defining an expert in science can become murky, as many professions engage in scientific practices. Yet, in this chapter we focus more on the practices of scientists, rather than the people themselves who may be called scientists. We see benefit in this perspective as it may be useful to a broader range of students as they consider how disciplinary literacy in science is applicable to them and their developing skills. Thus, to identify expert practices in science, we turn to the Scientific and Engineering Practices outlined in the Next Generation Science Standards (NGSS Lead States, 2013):

- Asking questions and defining problems
- Developing and using models
- Planning and carrying out investigations
- Analyzing and interpreting data
- Using mathematics and computational thinking

- Constructing explanations and designing solutions
- Engaging in argument from evidence
- Obtaining, evaluating, and communicating information

As you likely may recognize from reading the previous chapters about ELA and math, many practices overlap. This overlap is one factor in the way that we targeted Core Disciplinary Practices to think about how elementary students might best engage in disciplinary literacy. Table 7.1 considers these science practices relative to the Core Disciplinary Practices that are the focus of this book.

Notably, all of the practices described by the Next Generation Science Standards fall somewhere in one of the four Core Disciplinary Practices described in this book. Indeed, elementary teachers may find science one of the more approachable disciplines in their initial ventures into disciplinary literacy, as they already incorporate many disciplinary concepts and practices in science instruction. However, it may be that the disciplinary literacies are obscured or not explicitly taught in a way that would allow students to utilize those practices independently to support science learning. We also highlight that, just as in mathematics, text may be reconsidered in science to encompass a variety of artifacts that may be studied. Accordingly, science becomes a natural fit for analysis, comprehension, and communication from a disciplinary perspective.

What Role Do Digital Tools Play in Expert Science Practices?

As in other disciplines, scientists typically use a host of digital tools in their work. Often these tools are used in data collection and also in communicating results. Additionally, with more accessible advanced digital tools, such

Table 7.1. Connections Between Expert and Core Science Practices

Science Expert Practices	Core Disciplinary Practices
• Developing and using models • Planning and carrying out investigations	• Recognizing or comprehending multiple types of text
• Analyzing and interpreting data	• Analysis across multiple texts
• Asking questions and defining problems • Using mathematics and computational thinking	• Comprehending and using vocabulary particular to a discipline
• Constructing explanations and designing solutions • Engaging in argument from evidence • Obtaining, evaluating, and communicating information	• Developing and communicating ideas, arguments, or rationalizations

as virtual reality technology, experts increasingly are engaging in scientific study in virtual platforms. Table 7.2 illustrates more specifically the digital tools different types of scientists use and how these uses might translate to elementary disciplinary literacy instruction. Note these are a sampling of experts and not a comprehensive list.

As noted in previous chapters, this list is presented to help teachers to consider how digital tools may align with expert practices and bring the "real-world" aspect of science into the classroom to support elementary learners.

What Standards Promote Disciplinary Literacy in Science?

We used the Common Core State Standards in previous chapters to note commonalities between standards and Core Disciplinary Practices in English and mathematics. However, the CCSS do not include disciplinary standards for science (or social studies) for grades K–5. Thus, we turn again to the

Table 7.2. Expert Digital Tool Connections in Science

Experts	Examples of Professional Digital Tools	Possibilities for Classroom Application
Biologists Ecologists Zoologists	• Microscopes • Computer simulations • Speech-recognition audio tools • Camera	• Examining products from nature • Viewing digital simulations
Chemists	• Scales • Centrifuges • Digital learning models • Voice-activated assistants • Speech-recognition audio tools	• Using lab simulation apps for learners too young to handle extreme heat or freezing • Explaining experiment results or data using voice-recognition tools to support limited spelling knowledge
Geologists	• Digital compasses • Digital note-taking devices (tablets and computers) • Digital maps • Cameras	• Using digital cameras to document local geology • Identifying and labeling rocks and minerals using tablet apps for enhanced illustration
Astronomers	• Telescope • Spectrograph • Spacecrafts • Cameras • Computers	• Engaging in exploration with Google SkyView® Lite to stargaze from various locations on Earth

Next Generation Science Standards (NGSS Lead States, 2013). We focus on these standards as they are the most recent form of national standards available, with 26 states collaborating with the National Research Council, the National Science Teachers Association, and the American Association for the Advancement of Science to develop standards that provide students "an internationally benchmarked science education" (NGSS Lead States, 2013). Further, the NGSS (visit www.nextgenscience.org for examples) make direct connections to the CCSS for ELA and mathematics, aligning our intentions with previous disciplines discussed. Chapter 8 also will provide more specific examples of connections to the standards through lessons. As before, we provide Table 7.3 to draw direct connections between the language in the NGSS and Core Disciplinary Practices, to illustrate how the standards align with disciplinary literacy in elementary grades.

As you can see, the NGSS directly support disciplinary literacy in K–5, and all standards are focused on action in science. Starting in kindergarten, students are expected to read and understand multiple types of texts and data, use evidence and develop scientific descriptions that call for science vocabulary, and support and communicate arguments or explanations of scientific phenomena. These expectations directly align with Core Disciplinary Practices discussed in this book.

Selecting Texts for Disciplinary Literacy in Science

As we briefly noted previously, any object or scientific tool may be considered a text. A text, in general, is an artifact that can be read, studied, understood, and/or comprehended. Words may not necessarily be a feature of all texts, particularly in disciplines such as science. Yet, often teachers consider only the textbook or science-focused books to be texts. Science employs investigation and experimentation, which often places natural or biological artifacts at the center of literacy in science. Further, various text modalities are important to consider in elementary science text selection, as they often offer different pathways to understanding and support a range of learners (Cappello & Lafferty, 2015).

Digital texts and tools and multimodal representations of ideas are also of particular importance in science because many scientific ideas and phenomena are better observed than described. As Alvermann and Wilson (2011) stated, "Because science addresses different aspects of the physical universe, the observable properties and spatial arrangement of different entities are often essential for understandings of scientific content" (p. 118). Digital tools make it possible for scientists and teachers to create representations of scientific ideas that enable students to more easily understand concepts and make the content more accessible to a broader range of students.

Similarly, digital tools provide a way for students to represent their understanding of science content that may be difficult to describe or otherwise

Table 7.3. Connections Between NGSS Standards and Core Disciplinary Practices

Grade Level	Science NGSS
K	**K-PS3-1.** **Make observations** to determine **the effect** of sunlight on Earth's surface. **K-ESS2-2.** **Construct an argument supported by evidence** for how plants and animals (including humans) can change the environment to meet their needs.
1	**1-PS4-1.** **Plan and conduct investigations to provide evidence** that vibrating materials can make sound and that sound can make materials vibrate. **1-LS1-2.** **Read texts and use media to determine patterns** in behavior of parents and offspring that help offspring survive.
2	**2-LS2-2.** **Develop a simple model** that mimics the function of an animal in dispersing seeds or pollinating plants. **2-ESS2-1.** **Compare multiple solutions** designed to slow or prevent wind or water from changing the shape of the land.
3	**3-PS2-3.** **Ask questions to determine cause-and-effect** relationships of electric or magnetic interactions between two objects not in contact with each other. **3-LS3-1.** **Analyze and interpret data to provide evidence** that plants and animals have traits inherited from parents and that variation of these traits exists in a group of similar organisms.

communicate. Examples of digital tools that may support students' ability to comprehend and represent science ideas include 3-D printing and drawing, video tools for capturing examples or phenomena in action, and 360-degree videos that enable students to view environments with a 360-degree perspective. To guide the selection of texts that promote a wide range of science competencies for students, Table 7.4 takes a closer look at the Disciplinary Text Selection Table (Colwell, 2019) to consider appropriate texts in science and questions that may guide text selection.

Table 7.3. Connections Between NGSS Standards and Core Disciplinary Practices
(continued)

Grade Level	Science NGSS
4	**4-3SS3-2.** **Generate and compare multiple solutions** to reduce the impacts of natural Earth processes on humans. **4-PS3-4.** **Apply scientific ideas to design, test, and refine** a device that converts energy from one form to another.
5	**5-PS2-1.** **Support an argument** that the gravitational force exerted by Earth on objects is directed down. **5-ESS2-2.** **Describe and graph** the amounts of saltwater and fresh water in various reservoirs to **provide evidence** about the distribution of water on Earth.

Just as we highlighted in other discussions about disciplinary text selection, it is critical to select texts that not only attend to elementary students' various learning and literacy needs, but also support students in addressing culturally relevant approaches to disciplinary literacy in science. Science particularly promotes studying the world around us, bridging students'

Table 7.4. Modified Disciplinary Literacy Text Selection for Science

Print, Digital, and Other Multimodal Text Types	Questions to Consider
Diagrams (digital and nondigital) Graphs (digital and nondigital) Lab reports Photographs and images (digital and nondigital) Scientific proposals Natural artifacts (e.g., rocks, weather elements, leaves) Biological artifacts (e.g., cells, hair strands, etc.) 360-degree video (digital) 3-D printings (digital)	• Do the texts I selected address a relevant science-focused issue in society? • Do these texts represent a variety of formats to attend to students' various learning needs? • Are the scientific perspectives represented in the texts varied in perspective and background? • Can the scientific data represented in the texts be connected to students' culture and backgrounds? • What texts will students create to support scientific literacy? • What role will digital tools play in creating text? • How might digital tools better support students in creating disciplinary texts in science?

communities and personal lives with instruction, and text selection should mirror this opportunity. Additionally, digital texts that afford virtual opportunities and windows into scientific procedures and simulations that are not readily accessible may work to bridge socioeconomic disparities in how students study science and scientific texts.

HOW CAN DISCIPLINARY LITERACY INSTRUCTION BE DIGITALLY SUPPORTED IN SCIENCE?

As we have suggested, digital tools play a major role in the science discipline, both for experts and in supporting student learning through digital texts. We show in the next subsections the different ways in which disciplinary literacy can be digitally supported in science, with a particular focus on our core elementary disciplinary practices.

Recognizing and Comprehending Multiple Types of Science Texts

Just as in other elementary disciplines, it is important not only that students be able to comprehend different types of science texts but also that they recognize texts that are particular to the study of science. We see recognition and comprehension on a spectrum where students in early elementary grades focus more on recognizing science texts and gradually build comprehension skills as they move to upper grades. For example, a traditional lab report is far too complex for a kindergarten student to read or create. However, kindergarten students can recognize that science entails organized presentation of data focused on a specific question and can use digital tools to help them both read and present simple findings. Table 7.5 looks at other ways teachers might support students in this recognition and comprehension.

The 1st-grade and 5th-grade activities described here move students from basic identification of science texts, specifically in the identification of ocean life or analysis of a state's geological terrain. In 3rd grade, digital tools help students plan for a science experiment and then create a text that may provide evidence of more advanced understandings from the experiment, as students can talk their way through it rather than express their findings solely through writing. Ocean life, geological features of a region, and reports of experiment findings are all texts particular to various areas of science. Yet, they provide a different lens with which to promote and consider literacy in this discipline, while still aligning with grade-level science objectives and standards.

Analyzing Scientific Texts

Analysis of text is often a complex skill for many students, even in upper grades, and thus the level of analysis at which elementary students study

Table 7.5. Sample Literacy Strategies and Digital Tools to Support Recognition and Comprehension of Science Texts

Grade Level	Literacy Strategy	Digital Tool	Example
1	Preview	Digital simulation or virtual reality	Students take a digital fieldtrip of the ocean to identify different elements of aquatic life. Teachers can demonstrate how to take pictures so that students can capture and identify different fish, mammals, and plant life.
3	KWL	Podcast	Students identify and track what they know, what they want to know, and what they learned, critically considering a scientific question, conducting an experiment, and presenting results digitally through a podcast.
5	Jigsaw	Google Earth Digital annotation	Students work collaboratively in small groups to study the geological features of a region of the United States via Google Earth. Each group focuses on a particular state in the region and digitally annotates key geological features of that state. Students then share their digital annotations to consider the geology of the region as a whole.

texts is important to consider. While the types of texts scientists create are often in the form of reports or some type of model/simulation of findings, the texts that scientists study are often of living and inanimate objects that occur in nature or a laboratory. From an elementary literacy perspective, this actually may be a boon to disciplinary literacy in science, as traditional reading skills are often less of a consideration than in other disciplines where texts are word-based or numerical.

For example, a student's reading skills need not be advanced to study the effects of the seasons on the color and texture of tree foliage. Indeed, many preschool students begin experimenting and analyzing texts in science, with high levels of comprehension, long before they can read printed text. However, students at all elementary-grade levels require scaffolding in what to focus on in text analysis, how to organize findings from analysis of texts, and how to present findings in a scientifically appropriate manner. Digital tools may provide useful scaffolding for a variety of learners and grade levels, and we present Table 7.6 to provide examples and suggestions.

Table 7.6. Sample Literacy Strategies and Digital Tools to Support Analysis of Science Texts

Grade Level	Literacy Strategy	Digital Tool	Example
K	Think-aloud	Expert video clip	Teacher uses a video clip of a zoologist exploring and explaining a sun bear's natural habitat and how zoos try to replicate that habitat. The teacher pauses the clip at select points to stop and think aloud about how the zoo habitat compares with the natural habitat, based on the zoologist's explanation.
2	Study/observe-write-pair-share	Tablets/laptops Class digital sharing platform (e.g., Edmodo, Google classroom)	Students examine an in-class or virtual demonstration of water properties at varying temperatures to analyze properties in each temperature. Students record predictions before the demonstration, take notes during the demonstration (with a variety of languages and representations of thought allowed), and record findings afterward in a shared class document or discussion platform. Students then pair up to discuss the different comments in the document/platform after each temperature. Ideas then are shared aloud or with the comments feature in the platform.
4	Directed reading-thinking activity (DRTA)	Digital simulation	Students "read" (study) a digitally animated representation of plate tectonics and its effect on mountains and ocean trenches to consider, "What natural occurrences developed from tectonic plate movement?" They use a digital or print-based graphic organizer to take notes of predictions, what they learned during reading, and their conclusions.

We highlight how we move from group to more independent analysis as we progress in grade levels. Yet we do note that disciplinary analysis across grade levels remains dependent on visually and auditorily rich texts, as these types of texts better align with science texts, which are often heavy in graphics and support a larger variety of students. We also consider reading to be any act of studying, examining, or observing a science text, particularly as many science texts, as we have defined them in this book, do not consist of print-based words. Often existing instruction related to analysis focuses on print texts; however, a key disciplinary literacy practice of scientists is the use of a wide variety of materials when reading. For example, a scientific text may rely on graphs, figures, images, and links to other sources, and elementary students need to be prepared to analyze and integrate all of this information in order to generate understanding. This newer lens of reading directly influences vocabulary learning, which we turn to in the next section.

Using Vocabulary Particular to Science

Disciplinary literacy instruction in elementary grades offers a prime space for students to begin developing academic vocabulary as well as an awareness that each discipline has vocabulary that is unique (Shanahan & Shanahan, 2014). This awareness then begins to lay a foundation for appropriate use of science vocabulary. Additionally, science is often a subject where students learn that certain words, such as *base*, have different meanings depending on the discipline of focus.

A review of the Next Generation Science Standards and the Science and Engineering Practices contained therein reveals many disciplinary words and phrases that are essential for effective communication in science. Examples include words such as *patterns, models, conduct, investigation*, and *construct*. These words are likely to be familiar to many students, but may be used differently outside of a science context. Additionally, these are examples of words that are seen frequently in science across topics and grades. Thus, identifying, teaching, and reinforcing these types of words will help students build academic vocabulary knowledge needed to communicate about science through speaking, writing, listening, and producing multimodal and digital texts. As students are introduced to these words, the words can be added to a science word wall that includes images and other types of representations to reinforce the meaning of the words.

Table 7.7 provides an example of using a word wall strategy in science. In this table we have taken a slightly different approach from previous tables in this section to highlight how one literacy approach, word walls, may be integrated using a digital annotation tool to support students' disciplinary vocabulary in science in three different grade levels.

We focus on the word wall strategy across kindergarten, 2nd, and 4th grades as this is a common, if not staple, feature in many elementary classrooms to support vocabulary development. Also, we thought it might be useful to see how one literacy strategy can be modified and adapted as students' literacy and digital skills increase as they move through elementary grades. Using a digital tool, such as Padlet, that supports images, links, and videos allows students and teachers to create word walls that are more interactive, engaging, and supportive of differing literacy skills. Figure 7.1 presents an example of a Padlet word wall that might be found in a 2nd-grade classroom.

Table 7.7. Sample Literacy Strategy and Digital Tool to Support Science Vocabulary

Grade Level	Literacy Strategy	Digital Tool	Example
K			Teacher creates a class Padlet and posts images, links, and videos for disciplinary vocabulary related to plant parts.
2	Word wall	Annotated image tool (e.g., Padlet or Thinglink)	Teacher models and provides in-class opportunities to support students in posting and annotating images or videos to a class Padlet from a teacher-curated digital database related to ecosystem dynamics.
4			Students work in partners to locate, evaluate, and post to partner-created Padlets images, with accompanying annotations, related to properties of matter.

The manner in which the digital word wall is created, contributed to, used, and shared is dependent on the grade level, but the final product may better reach and support a variety of literacy learners. Thus, one digital tool and literacy strategy may support disciplinary vocabulary in multiple ways and contexts, with both teacher-centered and student-centered approaches to developing disciplinary vocabulary knowledge.

Communicating in Science

The final Core Disciplinary Practice of focus in science often aligns well as a target assessment for science lessons as teachers ask students to communicate and explain their findings in experiments or evaluations of science texts. We highlight in Table 7.8 how digital tools can support different literacy levels as elementary students are still developing their communication skills, both oral and written.

Teachers can use the literacy strategies and digital tools in Table 7.8 to consider how they might simultaneously support different levels of communication abilities and engagement with reflection, and build students' digital skills. Multiple digitally supported possibilities exist to help students more creatively explain their science learning while also helping them use skills that scientists use, such as reporting findings with evidence. Animated videos are low-risk and entertaining options for younger elementary students to explain findings orally and with graphic representations that might better express their learning than a word-based written task. RAFT writing is useful across K–12, but may be particularly important in mid-elementary

Figure 7.1. Padlet for 2nd-Grade Ecosystem Terms

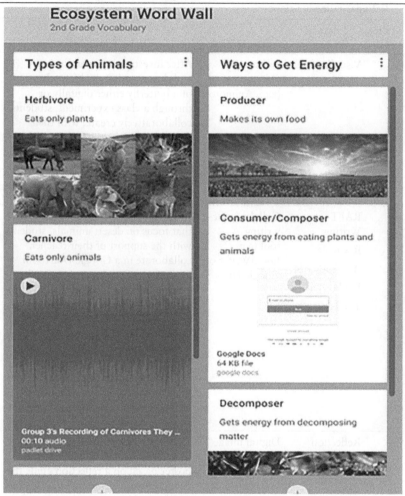

grades as students are moving to more content-focused and informational texts that are more difficult to read and interpret. Providing a scaffolded approach for students to step into the role of a scientist, such as an ecologist, and a structure for considering their writing, may lead to more successful experiences with disciplinary literacy in these transitional literacy years. Finally, we include a computer science connection, along with a digitally supported example, to highlight the multiple approaches that may be taken to help students communicate their disciplinary learning in different areas of science study, as they prepare to enter a secondary environment with a more disciplinary focus.

Table 7.8. Sample Literacy Strategies and Digital Tools to Communicate a Rationalization in Science

Grade Level	Literacy Strategy	Digital Tool	Example
1st	Visualization	Animated videos (e.g., Animoto)	After investigating, examining, and documenting the life cycle of a butterfly either digitally or through a class experiment, students collaboratively create, with their teacher and/or a partner, an animated video explaining the life cycle of a butterfly. Students' animated avatar could be a caterpillar or butterfly that discusses its metamorphosis.
3rd	RAFT Writing R = Role A = Audience F = Format T = Topic	Collaborative-writing tool (e.g., BoomWriter or Google Doc)	After studying multiple types of texts that focus on desert animals, students, with the support of their teacher, collaborate in a Google Doc to fill in sections of a lab report from the perspective of an ecologist studying common inherited traits of desert animals. The teacher helps students add in digital images and videos to create a multimodal report that may be viewed, listened to, and/or read. The class connects with another 3rd-grade class that examined inherited traits of wetland animals to compare and contrast findings.
5th	Reflection guide	Digital image presentation tool (e.g., Glogster)	Students work in small groups of 3–4 to create a multimedia digital poster based on a reflection guide they collaboratively generated that focuses on observable patterns based on the orbit of the Earth around the sun and of the moon around the Earth, along with Earth's rotation on its axis.
		Computer science connection coding app (e.g., ScratchJr)	After learning about a specific ecosystem through multiple types of texts, students work in pairs to build a similar type of ecosystem through coding to show relationships between plants, animals, and other environmental factors.

Practical Approaches to Digitally Supported Disciplinary Literacy in Science

As we have discussed in the previous chapter, science is a rich discipline that represents all of the Core Disciplinary Practices. In this chapter, however, we discuss approaches to the Core Disciplinary Practice of *Comprehending and Using Vocabulary Particular to a Discipline*. The language demands within science vary widely and range from terms with which students are already familiar, but that require a more precise semantic understanding, to highly technical classifications and processes. In the following lesson, we focus specifically on drawing on vocabulary instruction to support students in understanding the language practices within science. The lesson we reflect on is a common lesson about light and illumination in 1st grade to support both new terms, like *light wave*, and new understanding of existing terms, like *illumination* and *boundary*. In online Appendix C, we present a 4th-grade lesson about using natural resources for energy and the environmental effects of renewable and nonrenewable energy.

SAMPLE LESSON:
EVIDENCE-BASED ACCOUNT OF ILLUMINATION IN 1st GRADE

In this sample science lesson, we turn to the Next Generation Science Standards for guidance in integrating digitally supported disciplinary literacy into elementary instruction. In doing so, we highlight how 1st-grade teachers might focus on the Core Disciplinary Practice of *Comprehending and Using Vocabulary Particular to a Discipline* to teach light waves and illumination.

Phase 1: Identifying Appropriate Disciplinary Literacy Practices

This first phase of using the PEDDL Framework to support disciplinary literacy practices in science involves identifying the current standards guiding the lesson. The Next Generation Science Standards for 1st grade include standards related to physical science, life science, earth science, and engineering design. For this lesson, we have identified a typical physical science standard related to understanding light waves and illumination: "NGSS.1-PS4-2. Make observations to construct an evidence-based account that objects can be seen only when illuminated." This standard certainly relates to the Core Disciplinary Practice of *Communicating Ideas, Arguments, or Rationalizations*, and it is likely that existing instruction may support students' development in this area. Therefore, we focus instead on supporting students in recognizing how key vocabulary undergirds the development of evidence-based accounts in science, by targeting the Core Disciplinary Practice of *Comprehending and Using Vocabulary Particular to a Discipline*.

The existing lesson objectives draw on pictures and lights in the class to demonstrate the process of illumination, and ask students to recall why objects should be illuminated. While this is an important part of instruction related to the standard, it does not provide students with an opportunity to explain the process of illumination themselves, identify examples, or use vocabulary terms they may understand, but cannot yet write. For example, Figure 8.1 shows an example of a 1st-grade student's response to this lesson objective: "We can't see in the dark. So we can see them. Things can hide in the dark."

While it is clear from the example that the student understands some information about illumination, the response is not directly tied to a specific piece of evidence, and the lesson objective does not give students an opportunity to use vocabulary terms that may have been discussed as part of the classroom instruction. Envisioning a revised standard to support a more critical explanation would support students' development of understanding

Figure 8.1. Student Response to Original Objective

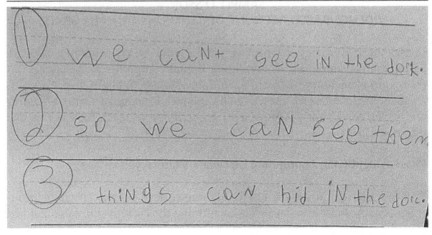

of how to use evidence to support conclusions and how to integrate precise scientific language into explanations. The revised standard also reflects increased precision in targeting specific parts of scientific knowledge to guide instruction. Without revisiting the complete description of the standard in the NGSS context, it might be possible to omit several dimensions of the standard that are important to both the scientific and disciplinary literacy knowledge. The revised learning objective specifies instruction related to objects that organically illuminate themselves and the influence of indirect light. This objective better captures the complexity of learning that happens within this standard, while still situating it within the bounds of 1st-grade instruction. It also utilizes some of the scientific terms related to this standard to support learning related to the science disciplinary practices connected to comprehending and understanding vocabulary. Table 8.1 shows these considerations in the PEDDL Framework.

Phase 2: Framing Disciplinary Literacy

In the next phase of the PEDDL Framework we consider how the revised objective supports students in identifying the importance of understanding illumination. Then, we consider how this understanding relates to practical matters of science outside of the classroom. The NGSS standard indicates that there is much to be known about why and how objects are illuminated and that students should understand this process. When thinking about why students need to know about illumination at all, we acknowledge that this is a tangible way for students to engage in the scientific method and to understand how professional scientists make observations and use specialized vocabulary in describing their processes and making claims.

In addition to understanding those ideas that relate to the nature of science (Draper & Adair, 2010), it is important to recognize that this is an opportunity for students to consider how understanding scientific processes not only allows them to better understand their world, but also prepares them to critically evaluate scientific information themselves. While many students have opportunities to collect data and make observations, it may not be clear to them that this better prepares them to understand and analyze data that others have collected and interpreted. Thus, the essential question guiding this lesson reflects calling attention to how understanding scientific processes can empower students to be critical producers and consumers of information.

Finally, after a review of the essential and enduring understandings related to this lesson, it becomes clear that a new objective is needed that specifically targets supporting student learning related to comprehending and using vocabulary. Without a learning objective related to vocabulary, students may miss a valuable opportunity to gain disciplinary knowledge about how language works in science.

Table 8.1. Planning Outline

Current Instructional Considerations	Disciplinary Extensions
PHASE 1: Identifying Appropriate Disciplinary Literacy Practices	
What state/national standards am I targeting?	What disciplinary practices are supported by those standards and objectives?
NGSS.1-PS4-2. Make observations to construct an evidence-based account that objects can be seen only when illuminated.	Comprehending and using vocabulary particular to a discipline
What are my lesson objectives?	
Original objective: After observing several items in a state of darkness and light, students will be able to list 2–4 reasons why objects need to be illuminated.	
Revised objectives after adding disciplinary extensions: Students will understand and provide 3–4 authentic examples of illuminated objects, including at least one organic and one indirect light example, and describe how the light source works in each example.	
PHASE 2: Framing Disciplinary Literacy	
What information is important for my students to learn and understand from this lesson?	Why is it important for students to learn and understand this topic?
Objects need to be illuminated to be seen, and there are many different ways for objects to be illuminated, including objects that give off their own light or that can be illuminated through indirect light sources.	While most students are aware that they cannot see things in the dark, they may not understand how light functions to illuminate objects, and related concepts such as boundaries, transparency, shadow, and light waves. This is a tangible way to support students in understanding how scientists study the world and how communicating about scientific topics utilizes a specialized vocabulary. An important goal of science instruction is to prepare students to develop evidence-based understanding of phenomena and the role that language can play in understanding scientific concepts. Therefore, the essential question for this lesson is:
	Why is it important to understand how processes in nature work and to be able to explain those processes to others?

Table 8.1. Planning Outline (*continued*)

Current Instructional Considerations	Disciplinary Extensions
PHASE 3: Selecting Multimodal Texts for Disciplinary Literacy	
What texts does my school or school district require when teaching this topic? No materials provided	What digital and multimodal texts might supplement my currently used texts and extend students' learning to encourage disciplinary literacy?
What texts do I feel comfortable using to support students' learning? Which topical texts align with my students' current reading levels? A class set of *All About Light* by Lisa Trumbauer (2004) and a collection of flashlights	Videos of natural phenomena that cannot be created in the classroom Instructional videos that diagram the process of illumination How might these digital and multimodal texts help support students to engage in more advanced reading, writing, and communication practices? Through engaging students with a variety of print types and scientific ways to communicate information, students will have a wider repertoire of scientific tools and language to draw upon.
PHASE 4: Assessing Disciplinary Literacy with a Variety of Tools	
What assessments do I currently use to determine students' learning and understanding of this topic? Short writing	How can I incorporate digital tools to further assess students' understanding of disciplinary practices and texts?
What type(s) of knowledge (e.g., fact-based, process-based, etc.) do those assessments gauge? Fact-based knowledge	Incorporating a digital audio recorder tool (e.g., Chatterpix) where students can record their voices enables students to use complex vocabulary that may be too difficult to write. This also supports students in their ability to communicate evidence-based accounts, a critical science disciplinary practice. How do these digital tools create or support a more comprehensive assessment of students' understanding? Using a digital audio recorder tool allows students to not be confined to only terms and ideas they know how to briefly list. Further, by having students use the audio recorder tool to discuss digital image examples of illumination, the teacher is also able to evaluate process knowledge and identify areas where students may need additional conceptual support. This provides a more comprehensive assessment of disciplinary understanding than just checking to ensure the facts listed are correct.

Table 8.1. Planning Outline *(continued)*

Current Instructional Considerations	Disciplinary Extensions
PHASE 5: Digitally Supporting Disciplinary Literacy Instruction	
How do I prepare my students to learn this topic? Discussion of dark and light Use of physical examples in the classroom	What digital tools extend and deepen students' preparation to learn this topic? Inclusion of videos can allow for curating a number of examples of living and nonliving objects, and for including discussion of boundaries and light waves, which are not easily created with manipulatives and print texts.
How do I guide my students' comprehension of this topic? Ask questions after each example. Read the book *All About Light* by Lisa Trumbauer (2004) and explain each example. How do I help my students reflect on their learning of this topic? Students determine whether their answers on the assessment match the reasons discussed in class.	What digital tools support and extend students' synthesis of learning in this topic? What digital tools support students' development of artifacts to illustrate disciplinary literacy? Chatterpix allows students to select images that show illumination and to record themselves explaining the illumination process at work. An important disciplinary practice is using original evidence, like the image, and then clearly explaining the processes at work, the illumination.
PHASE 6: Reflecting to Reach All Learners	
How have I differentiated instruction in this lesson? Students can work in a number of ways with the flashlights. There is a wide range of differentiation available in the images students choose and what they say in their explanations.	How have I considered personal, social, and cultural understandings that inform this lesson? Students are invited into the disciplinary practices of scientists to understand why we need to be able to consider evidence and draw conclusions independently. Additionally, drawing on students' own lives, and then extending the examples into contexts outside of what is familiar to them, enable students to understand how illumination is a common thread throughout personal, social, and cultural experiences.

Phase 3: Selecting Multimodal Texts for Disciplinary Literacy

Unlike for literacy and math, many elementary schools do not utilize a comprehensive curriculum for science instruction. Therefore, the process of evaluating existing materials in Phase 3 may entail looking at a particular grade-level science kit or simply identifying available resources within the classroom. In this lesson, we identify some common manipulatives and a popular text about light as the existing materials.

The text *All About Light* by Lisa Trumbauer (2004) is a useful existing resource that can serve to introduce students to vocabulary involved in understanding light waves through exploring images and concepts with which they are already familiar. Students then can practice these concepts with manipulatives, experimenting with how flashlights work in their classroom to begin to explore the boundaries and distance that light waves can travel and still illuminate objects.

However, animated diagrams and explanations of this process not only would support students' depth of understanding of the process of illumination, but also would represent more closely how scientists model and interpret data. Further, watching organically illuminated objects, such as animals in the ocean whose cells trigger bioluminescence at dusk, can situate this concept in new contexts that extend beyond what may already be familiar to students. Teachers can capitalize on these new contexts to showcase different terms used to talk about light, depending on where the light comes from.

A wide variety of digital materials related to illumination are available that will allow teachers to differentiate their instruction for students along a number of factors. Students also can work together in groups to question and discuss the illumination described in multiple videos in order to determine common elements that describe why objects must be illuminated to be seen. The process of identifying instructional materials and considering how multimodal texts may support students' understanding of disciplinary practices in science is shown in Table 8.1.

Phase 4: Assessing Disciplinary Literacy with a Variety of Tools

An assessment such as short writing may no longer meet the disciplinary goals of this lesson. Because it places emphasis on disciplinary vocabulary in science, this type of assessment is unlikely to accurately gauge 1st-grade students' more sophisticated understanding of complex terms that they may not be able to write. Yet, by revising the assessment, teachers may be able to gain a more robust understanding of students' science and vocabulary knowledge.

For example, a digital tool, such as the Chatterpix app, that incorporates images with students' recorded voices allows students to provide specific evidence of illumination and orally explain it through recording their own voices. This provides students the opportunity to not only meet the learning objectives, but also practice the important science disciplinary practice of basing explanation on specific pieces of evidence.

Teachers also may be able to more accurately identify specific places where any misconceptions or misunderstandings have occurred because the assessment involves multiple steps. For example, students who have selected an image that does not explicitly show an object being illuminated, may not understand the vocabulary concept of illumination. Therefore, students may not be able to utilize the vocabulary associated with this concept, which may identify an opportunity for additional instruction or practice with specific terms. This assessment has multiple opportunities for teachers to better understand student learning about illuminating objects.

Phase 5: Digitally Supporting Disciplinary Literacy Instruction

In Phase 5, we aim to demonstrate how digitally supported disciplinary literacy instruction can support and extend existing classroom instruction. In this example, there are existing materials that contribute important elements of instruction to students' learning why objects need to be illuminated to be seen. Using flashlights in the classroom is an important kinesthetic experience for understanding illumination and boundaries of light. We would add that scientists often return to data as they understand more about a phenomenon. Thus, rather than just using the flashlights and classroom lights in the beginning of the lesson, we use these as touchstone activities for students to return to as they learn more about light waves and illuminating objects. Additionally, the text *All About Light* is useful, as students can have their own copy during this lesson and refer to the examples.

However, this text is limited in the breadth of discussion and types of examples provided. Inviting students to consider how objects are illuminated in their own lives, and showing image examples of objects that are not part of students' daily lives, are important ways to both connect learning to students' own cultures as well as broaden their understanding outside of their own lives. This reflects the scientific disciplinary practice of creating generalizable knowledge, or knowledge that would hold true in multiple circumstances. Thus, inclusion of digital images would support the learning objectives as well as help students gain experience in the disciplinary literacy of science.

The digital tool selected for this lesson, Chatterpix, is useful for synthesizing the multiple types of learning and disciplinary practices involved in the lesson. It allows students to demonstrate knowledge of familiar and unfamiliar objects through including digital images as their evidence and to use the science-specific vocabulary in their narrated explanations. Additionally, these types of platforms are easy to use, fun, and engaging for young children, as they can make any type of object "talk" with students' own voice

Figure 8.2. Chatterpix Photo Showing Illumination in an Aquarium

recording. A screenshot of a Chatterpix photo explaining how light illuminates a class aquarium is shown in Figure 8.2.

Notice, too, that we focused on using digital tools only to prepare students for learning and to help them in reflection. As seen in other lesson examples, it is unnecessary to force digital tools throughout instruction. Instead, we look for ways to enhance disciplinary literacy instruction with digital tools to support all learners and then consider the appropriate points in instruction to integrate the tools.

Phase 6: Reflecting to Reach All Learners

In the final phase of the PEDDL Framework we consider how all of the elements of the lesson work together to support all learners and then extend that reflection to how students gain enduring understanding from the instruction. In this lesson, reconsideration of existing instructional activities allows them to be more differentiated, as students are able to return to the flashlights and classroom lights as touchstone activities to support additional learning.

Through reflective analysis of the revised lesson, a stronger connection to personal, social, and cultural understandings that relate to the lesson objectives is revealed. Students have more choice in the way that they represent their knowledge, which involves consideration of the ways in which the topic of illumination connects to their personal lives as well as those of people in very different places and circumstances.

QUESTIONS TO PONDER

1. The types of vocabulary discussed here seem different from the vocabulary lists we usually use. Should I focus only on scientific vocabulary?

No. Elementary students are still building critical foundational vocabulary, so, unlike vocabulary instruction in secondary grades, stopper words (i.e., unknown words that cause students to stop reading) should still be addressed and assessed. However, by incorporating key scientific vocabulary, such as *illumination* and *state of darkness*, and having students engage in activities that help them understand these more complex scientific concepts, teachers enable students to consider that different types of vocabulary exist.

2. Will my grading time increase if I have to watch all of my students' videos?

Not necessarily. In fact, many teachers who frequently use audio-recording tools find it easier to respond to students orally using an accompanying audio app or program. These types of feedback techniques often require less time than providing written feedback. For example, with Chatterpix, teachers can create a quick 30-second feedback image to send directly to students. Bonus: Students love to hear their teachers speak directly to them!

3. How do I support students who feel uncomfortable with oral communication?

Have students write out or jot notes on the text they plan to record. You can even provide a type of fillable script or outline that students can use as a guide to structure their disciplinary learning and vocabulary use.

After considering these questions, we hope you turn next to the additional science lesson provided in Appendix C online, which looks at planning digitally supported disciplinary literacy instruction in 4th-grade science. In it, the same Core Disciplinary Practice of *Comprehending and Using Vocabulary Particular to a Discipline* is targeted, along with a second Core Disciplinary Practice (i.e., *Obtaining, Evaluating, and Communicating Information*) to consider the possibility of focusing on two complementary Core Disciplinary Practices in an upper-level elementary grade.

Examining Disciplinary Literacy in Elementary Social Studies

Third grade offers a wealth of concepts to cover in social studies, and Ms. Branch is eager to think about ways that disciplinary literacy might be a part of her instruction in this area. She worries because there are a variety of reading and learning levels among her students and she knows that, from a history perspective, social studies texts can be intimidating with the sometimes formal or less-common language found in primary sources. However, she knows that geography also plays a large role in social studies and offers fewer word-based texts to study. In fact, map-based skills in world history and geography is a key area of focus in the standards for her state. To address both history and geography, Ms. Branch decides to plan a lesson on understanding the culture and geography of ancient China. She searches the Internet and her school's professional library for digital resources that might provide students with interactive opportunities to engage with a map of China. She locates a digital, interactive map of ancient China with corresponding leveled texts and audio to use as one of her texts. To supplement and expand students' thinking about the geography of ancient China and its effects on economy and history, she provides students with images from that time period so that students may read across sources and study that time more closely than they could with solely their textbook.

INTEGRATING DISCIPLINARY LITERACY INTO SOCIAL STUDIES

Social studies can be a complex discipline to tackle from an elementary standpoint, as multiple subdisciplines, that is, civics, economics, geography, and history, are targeted in curricula. Once students enter middle and high school grades, these four subdisciplines become more distinguished and are often separate classes. However, at the K–5 levels of instruction, history is often the focus of state standards, with civics, economics, and geography being supporting subdisciplines. Nevertheless, each subdiscipline plays an important role in students' social studies learning, and we discuss each area specifically throughout this chapter. To do so, we first present an overview of the skills required for disciplinary literacy in the subdisciplines of social studies and then address, as in previous chapters, how these skills might look in K–5 instruction.

History

To be literate in history, students need to develop literacy skills related to studying multiple sources of information, considering the source and context of the information, and then corroborating what they learned from studying these different sources (Wineburg, 1991, 2001). Studying different types of text is also important, and teachers should present an array of texts to students in history instruction to develop disciplinary literacy skills. Often history instruction focuses on the memorization of facts and dates, and although historical facts and dates are important for context, students must be able to use them in a larger investigation of primary sources to address an overarching, essential question, such as, "Is war necessary?" In focusing a social studies lesson on broad, but important, questions relevant to real-life inquiry, civics, economics, and geography can all become important areas of study as well.

Civics

In civics, students should understand both how to apply the rules of a democratic society to everyday life and the rationale behind those rules. Students must be able to rationalize their decisions with relevant and trustworthy information, and know how to determine the source and reliability of that information. They should be able to consider civic virtues and to take different perspectives (a) to understand why people make the decisions they do, and (b) to inform their own choices and actions that support the good of society. In grades K–5, civic virtues such as voting and volunteering should be introduced, and students should be given opportunities to think about how these civic virtues relate to a larger role in society, particularly in times of war. Indeed, these skills are outlined specifically in the C3 Framework (NCSS, 2013), which we address in a following section. Also, as citizenship and civic competence has become an increasingly relevant goal in today's society and in the education of young people (Pennington, Obenchain, & Brock, 2014), civics becomes an important subdiscipline in social studies.

Economics

Economics, although often seen as an advanced topic, can be an exciting and engaging way for students to understand how we obtain goods and products and how we pay for services. In K–5 instruction, where economics has more of a minor focus, it also can be beneficial to have students study history from an economic standpoint to understand bartering and rationales behind topics such as war, world exploration, and power.

Geography

Geography also can be taught in the context of history as students think about the role of regional inhabitants and atmosphere in historical events such as war. Continuing with our example essential question, "Is war necessary?" the topography of a region also can be important in helping students understand strengths and vulnerability in war. From a disciplinary perspective in geography, maps of regions become resources students engage in and study as integrally linked with major world events, rather than rote memorization, such as learning capitals.

Therefore, in social studies, disciplinary literacy provides opportunities to make learning more meaningful by supporting an inquiry-based approach. Such an approach strengthens thinking and inquiry skills that students may use outside of the classroom as well as provides a foundation for more advanced disciplinary skills students will use in future middle and high school grades.

Who Are Social Studies Experts and What Do They Practice?

As we recognize that social studies is a core content area in K–5 education, but note that it consists of various subdisciplines, we turn to consideration of experts and expert practices in each of these subdisciplines. Specifically, the *College, Career, and Civic Life (C3) Framework for Social Studies State Standards* (NCSS, 2013) focuses on the four subdisciplines of civics, economics, geography, and history to illustrate disciplinary expert practices and how they may be framed for social studies instruction. The NCSS (2013) suggests concepts, skills, and disciplinary tools necessary to engage in social studies learning and prepare students for college, career, and civic life, which may be supported by an Inquiry Arc that outlines four ideas related to expert practices in social studies:

- Developing questions and planning inquiries
- Applying disciplinary concepts and tools
- Evaluating sources and using evidence
- Communicating conclusions and taking informed action (p. 17)

We highlight the practices outlined in the C3 Framework, which was prepared by a team of social studies educators and scholars focused on developing a standards-based framework in which disciplinary practices are the focus of social studies instruction. Specifically, this framework was developed to support and align with the Common Core State Standards for Social Studies/History (Herczog, 2010).

Notably, the C3 Framework highlights that each subdiscipline has multiple types of experts. In civics alone, a variety of government officials, politicians, police officers or officers of any type of security agency, along with scholars who study civics and political science, may be considered experts. Accordingly, we constructed Table 9.1 to outline the many experts in social studies, organized by subdisciplines, and briefly describe their practices.

Primarily, we draw attention to the idea that all expert practices across the field of social studies take into consideration multiple sources of data to inform larger decisions and understandings about a topic. Also, students must be able to consider a source of information, and who developed or created that source, to better inform whether it is reliable and must be able to use vocabulary associated with those sources. Thus, in social studies, all four Core Disciplinary Practices may be applicable across subdisciplinary expert practices. These practices will be expanded on in later subsections.

What Role Do Digital Tools Play in Expert Social Studies Practices?

Although multiple subfields exist in social studies, commonly used digital tools may be found across disciplines. In part, this is because social studies is, in essence, the examination of society. When studying humans and factors that affect the world humans inhabit, digital tools that capture society-focused data or that present data from the past are important. Particularly, we focus on the ways that experts in social studies may use digital tools to record data, to study multiple sources of data, and to explain their findings. Table 9.2 highlights sample experts, the digital tools they use, and possibilities for classroom application in elementary grades.

We provide these examples to help teachers consider how they may explain to students the ways that experts use digital tools. Additionally, it may be beneficial for teachers to consider how such tools may support students in either expert practices or practices that lay a foundation for these practices. Chapter 10 provides a concrete example of what these practices might look like in an elementary classroom.

What Standards Promote Disciplinary Literacy in Social Studies?

Just as we discussed in Chapter 7 in regard to disciplinary literacy in science, social studies is not targeted in the Common Core State Standards until 6th grade. Nevertheless, there is a national focus on promoting common disciplinary practices in social studies beginning in kindergarten. Therefore, we turn again to the C3 Framework for Social Studies Standards, developed by the National Council for Social Studies (2013). These standards are based on the 2010 National Curriculum Standards for social studies.

Table 9.1. Connections Between Expert and Core Social Studies Practices

Sub-discipline	Experts	Expert Practices	Core Disciplinary Practices
Civics	• Civics and political science scholars • Government officials • Politicians • Lawyers • Police or security-related officers	• Determining, enforcing, or critiquing rules and guidelines for a civilized society • Rationalizing and reasoning the law	• Recognizing or comprehending multiple types of text • Analysis across multiple texts • Comprehending and using vocabulary particular to a discipline • Developing and communicating ideas, arguments, or rationalizations
Economics	• Economists • Economics scholars/professors • Government advisors and consultants on resources • Business analysts	• Analysis of production and consumption of goods based on supply and demand • Forecasting or theorizing economic outlook based on multiple data	
Geography	• Geographers • Geography scholars/professors	• Analysis of physical and human characteristics of a region to inform history, politics, and natural phenomena	
History	• Historians • Historical scholars/professors	• Analysis of past evidence to understand events and timelines • Sourcing primary texts and information • Contextualizing primary sources • Corroborating findings across sources of information	

Table 9.2. Expert Digital Tool Connections in Social Studies

Expert	Examples of Professional Digital Tools	Possibilities for Classroom Application
Lawyer Police officer or law agent	• Digital databases (court rulings, forensic evidence, criminal records) • Digital recording tools for interviews	• Using digital tools for peer-to-peer or peer-to-relative/friend interviews
Economist	• Digital databases of historical data to inform economic outlooks • Digital graphing tools • Analytical software	• Examining sales/trade data from history to form interpretations • Creating digital graphs to illustrate economic predictions
Geographer	• Global Positioning System • Satellite images • Google Maps/digital maps • Digital charts and graphs • Geographical Information Systems (GIS)	• Using Google Maps or satellite images to study regional landscapes
Historian	• Digital online archives of historical data • Digital library-supported databases • Digital cameras	• Using digital cameras to document local history • Analyzing historical digital photographs and digital recordings to form interpretations of an event in history

These standards differ from other content areas discussed in this book because they are not content-driven, but instead were developed to support states in aligning their content with principles that target holistic themes pertinent to social studies. As such, the practices promoted in the standards cut across states' social studies curricula, providing a national perspective when considering how social studies standards promote disciplinary literacy in grades K–5.

Thus, these standards serve as a building block to the social studies/history CCSS, which begin in 6th grade. And, they are organized by the four dimensions of the Inquiry Arc described previously. However, the C3 Framework standards are not specific to each individual grade level. Instead, they are driven by what students should know by the end of 2nd, 5th, 8th, and 12th grades. Thus, we focus here on specifically what students should know and be able to do in social studies by the end of 2nd grade and 5th grade, organized by the four Inquiry Arc dimensions. Table 9.3 connects these standards to disciplinary literacy in the elementary grades, along with the Core Disciplinary Practices of focus in this book.

Table 9.3. Connections Between C3 Framework for Social Studies Standards and Core Disciplinary Practices

Dimension	C3 Framework for Social Studies Standards	
	By the End of 2nd Grade	*By the End of 5th Grade*
1. Developing questions and planning inquiries	**D1.2.K-2.** Identify disciplinary ideas associated with a compelling question. **D1.5.K-2.** Determine the kinds of sources that will be helpful in answering compelling and supporting questions.	**D1.2.3-5.** Identify disciplinary concepts and ideas associated with a compelling question that are open to different interpretations. **D1.4.3-5.** Explain how supporting questions help answer compelling questions in an inquiry.
2. Applying disciplinary concepts and tools	**D2.Civ.10.K-2.** Compare their own point of view with others' perspectives. **D2.Eco.14.K-2.** Describe why people in one country trade goods and services with people in other countries. **D2.Geo.1.K-2.** Construct maps, graphs, and other representations of familiar places. **D2.His.11.K-2.** Identify the maker, date, and place of origin for a historical source from information within the source itself.	**D2.Civ.14.3-5.** Illustrate historical and contemporary means of changing society. **D2.Eco.6.3-5.** Explain the relationship between investment in human capital, productivity, and future incomes. **D2.Geo.10.3-5.** Explain why environmental characteristics vary among different world regions. **D2.His.10.3-5.** Compare information provided by different historical sources about the past.

(table continues on next page)

Table 9.3. Connections Between C3 Framework for Social Studies Standards and Core Disciplinary Practices *(continued)*

Dimension	C3 Framework for Social Studies Standards	
	By the End of 2nd Grade	*By the End of 5th Grade*
3. Evaluating sources and using evidence	**D3.1.K-2.** Gather relevant information from one or two sources while using the origin and structure to guide the selection. **D3.2.K-2.** Evaluate a source by distinguishing between **fact and opinion.**	**D3.3.3-5.** Identify evidence that draws information from multiple sources in response to compelling questions. **D3.4.3-5.** Use evidence to develop claims in response to compelling questions.
4. Communicating conclusions and taking informed action	**D4.1.K-2.** Construct an argument with reasons. **D4.8.K-2.** Use listening, consensus-building, and voting procedures to decide on and take action in their classrooms.	**D4.4.3-5.** Critique arguments. **D4.6.3-5.** Draw on disciplinary concepts to explain the challenges people have faced and opportunities they have created in addressing local, regional, and global problems at various times and places.

We encourage teachers to further explore these standards, if unfamiliar, to see firsthand how they build on one another and to strategically scaffold disciplinary practices from kindergarten through 12th grade. Additionally, Dimension 2 is broken down into the subdisciplines of civics, economics, geography, and history, providing far more standards than we could illustrate here.

Further, social studies, like English language arts, entails much word-based reading, and some disciplinary practices are unsuitable for students who are still learning to read. For example, there are dimensions, such as evaluating sources and using evidence, that do not list standards until grades 3–5, as the practices associated with these dimensions of social studies learning are too complex for early elementary learners. Unlike ELA, primary sources are not leveled for young readers and often reflect the language norms of a time period or of experts. Thus, it may be more difficult to engage young elementary students in disciplinary practices in some subdisciplines of social studies. However, we encourage teachers to consider the practices that are appropriate and to remember that some K–2 practices, such as identifying the maker, date, and place of a historical source, provide foundational skills for future disciplinary literacy. Additionally, a range of texts may be used in social studies, some of which are not word-based, and may help students engage in standards-driven disciplinary literacy even before they have mastered word-based reading.

Selecting Texts for Disciplinary Literacy in Social Studies

Indeed, a myriad of texts may be found in the social studies disciplines. We find this variety of texts a strength of integrating disciplinary literacy in K–5 as teachers have a host of texts to choose from. Digital archives also offer recordings that are audio- and/or video-based, drawings and photographs, and maps with digital features to enhance "readability," which may support text comprehension for younger elementary students and many different learning levels. We take a final look in Table 9.4 at the Disciplinary Text Selection Table (Colwell, 2019) to expand it for considering digital texts and questions that guide the integration of multimodal texts into social studies.

Social studies, in particular, offers ripe opportunities to select texts that afford students not only digital learning opportunities but opportunities to

Table 9.4. Modified Disciplinary Literacy Text Selection for Social Studies

Print, Digital, and Other Multimodal Text Types	Questions to Consider
• Laws • Civic responsibilities • Civic dispositions • Surveys • Trade reports and charts • Production reports and charts • Maps • Demographic data • Speeches • Letters • Photographs • Advertisements • Political cartoons • Oral histories • Videos/film	• Am I selecting more than one text for students to use in corroborating information? • If I am selecting only one text, can the text be analyzed for source information? • Am I selecting different types and modalities of texts, sources, and text formats? • Do the texts represent a variety of perspectives and voices? • Do the voices represented in the texts reflect similar cultures and backgrounds to those of my students? • What text features are present that will support students in comprehension? • Will a digital version of the text potentially offer additional support? • What texts will students create to illustrate their disciplinary literacy?

consider a variety of perspectives that may shape more culturally aware learners. As the text examples suggest, multiple types of societal, cultural, and historical viewpoints may be represented in social studies texts, providing a launch pad for engaged learning and discussion about relevant real-world ideas. We certainly believe these viewpoints may be found in any of the disciplines discussed in this book. Yet, creating better-informed citizens is an encompassing goal in social studies, and offering students, beginning in the early grades, the opportunity to learn about different world and social views is a unique and exciting aspect of social studies instruction.

HOW CAN DISCIPLINARY LITERACY INSTRUCTION BE DIGITALLY SUPPORTED IN SOCIAL STUDIES?

We now turn to our Core Disciplinary Practices in elementary grades and how they may be integrated into social studies, using digital tools and texts. As there are four subdisciplines, we aim to address each of them as equally as possible throughout the entirety of this section. Thus, not every subdiscipline will be discussed in each core practice, but we do focus on multiple subdisciplines in each Core Disciplinary Practice to convey the manner in which these practices translate across social studies.

Recognizing and Comprehending Multiple Types of Social Studies Texts

Just as social studies is a diverse discipline with its multiple subdisciplines, the texts that can be considered social studies texts are equally diverse, as described in a previous section. Especially for students in grades K–2, it may be most beneficial to focus on recognition of texts that would normally be considered social studies texts. In grades 3–5, students may venture further into reading, analyzing, and comprehending different types of social studies texts, and, particularly in 4th and 5th grades, reading across texts to draw conclusions based on evidence. Table 9.5 considers three different grade levels and how literacy strategies and digital tools might be used to scaffold disciplinary learning.

Analyzing Social Studies Texts

As students gain confidence with comprehending and recognizing social studies texts, they also should be supported in the analysis of those texts. Analysis of social studies texts at the elementary level positions students to build skills related to inferencing and reading across texts, skills that are needed in all of the subdisciplines of social studies. Table 9.6 depicts how specific literacy strategies and digital tools can support students' learning of social studies content, as well as developing an understanding of the disciplinary literacies of social studies.

Table 9.5. Sample Literacy Strategies and Digital Tools to Support Recognition and Comprehension of Social Studies Texts

Grade Level	Literacy Strategy	Digital Tool	Example
1st	Using a graphic organizer to organize different historical images	Various websites Digital graphic organizer to copy and paste pictures	The teacher guides students to explore different digital images of Pocahontas, found through a teacher-guided Internet search, to distinguish between historical and fictional representations of the historical figure, sorting images digitally in a graphic organizer.
3rd	Annotation	Digital version of a historical document	Students work collaboratively in groups or pairs to read the National Archives digital version of the *Bill of Rights* that uses plain language to explain each of the 10 Amendments.
5th	Questioning the Author (Beck, McKeown, Hamilton, & Kucan, 1997).	Digital recordings of a historical speech	Students listen to a digital recording of Dr. Martin Luther King's "I Have a Dream" speech and create time-stamped queries either digitally or on paper for a closer analysis of Dr. King's message.

Table 9.6. Sample Literacy Strategies and Digital Tools to Support Analysis of Social Studies Texts

Grade Level	Literacy Strategy	Digital Tool	Example
K	Preview	Interactive topographic digital map	The teacher navigates a topographic digital map of the region in which students live to introduce students to the different features of their geographical area.
2nd	Anticipation guide	Digital resource archive	Students explore photographs on the National Geographic Kids website and respond to prompts in a teacher-created anticipation guide regarding cultural comparisons across the globe.
5th	Close reading	Leveled primary source website (e.g., Newsela)	Students engage in close reading of primary sources regarding the American Revolution through Newsela, which adjusts the language to suit younger students' learning and literacy abilities.

These strategies not only support students in utilizing multiple modes of texts, but also provide a foundation for considering the more critical aspects of social studies disciplinary literacy involving perspectives, accuracy of accounts and information, differing perspectives, and social and cultural implications of information. Providing structured support for students to build their own analytical skills can bolster their understanding of analysis of social studies texts.

Using Vocabulary Particular to Social Studies

The range of vocabulary demands within social studies is wide, from the historical vernacular of some primary sources to mathematical economics and scientific geography language. All of these terms require domain-specific instruction, as students must understand these terms in order to comprehend social studies texts. Key to vocabulary instruction in social studies is to recognize the specific words and language patterns that students may need to know in order to analyze a text. For example, understanding the specific meaning of the word *cabinet*, a key term in studies of government, requires instruction to introduce a new context for an already familiar word. That term itself is not particularly challenging but requires an understanding of context in order to understand the definition in social studies. Vocabulary instruction also extends into exploring the relationships among words as an especially important part of accessing primary sources. Table 9.7 illustrates examples from 1st, 3rd, and 5th grades for utilizing literacy strategies to explore relationships among words and develop word knowledge within social studies.

These strategies build students' capabilities in both recognizing the disciplinary language used in the subdisciplines of history, as well as understanding how language works within different types of social studies texts. The strategies shown in Table 9.7 highlight the increasing complexity and sophistication that students are able to engage in as they become more confident with vocabulary and word knowledge in their foundational literacy.

Communicating in Social Studies

In social studies, being able to communicate about texts is critical to students' abilities to make independent claims about ideas and explain them to others. Because social studies experts so often are called upon to develop new ideas based on synthesizing multiple perspectives, communicating about social studies concepts is an important element in disciplinary literacy practices.

Table 9.7. Sample Literacy Strategies and Digital Tools to Support Social Studies Vocabulary

Grade Level	Literacy Strategy	Digital Tool	Example
1st	Shared reading	Images of different local and national leaders	Students will read about people who lead U.S. governmental structures, like mayor, governor, and president. They will view and interpret images of their local mayor and governor to compare local- and national-level leaders.
3rd	Word wall	Digital map creator	Students will utilize geographical terms such as the cardinal directions, latitude and longitude, and map key to develop a map of a fictional place to show understanding of map terms.
5th	Semantic feature analysis	Digital images Digital document	Students create a semantic feature analysis chart of different processes related to making a law. The chart can include images and links to authentic documents to demonstrate differences.

We emphasize that social studies experts communicate in a variety of ways, and students should have opportunities to communicate orally, in written form, and through the design of multimedia communication. This can begin as early as kindergarten, where students would be able to record their interpretations of narratives that are read to them or videos they watch.

An additional part of communicating in social studies is to understand the different rhetorical approaches utilized by the different subdisciplines. While students may not begin by producing rationalizations themselves, careful attention to the structure of communication is an important part of scaffolding students' abilities to create and communicate effectively in the social studies domain. Table 9.8 provides examples of how to support students' ability to communicate in social studies.

These strategies not only serve to support student understanding of the disciplinary literacies of social studies, but also utilize authentic communication practices within the various subdisciplines. Thus, students gain early experience with communicating and producing rationalizations and arguments that relate directly to the various ways that social studies experts communicate their own conclusions and understandings.

Table 9.8. Sample Literacy Strategies and Digital Tools to Communicate a Rationalization in Social Studies

Grade Level	Literacy Strategy	Digital Tool	Example
K	Kinesthetic role play	Digital examples of multiple types of currency; audio-recording or podcasting tool	Students will use currency to demonstrate an understanding of money and trading through creating a good and trading within the class. They will then explore currency in multiple cultures and explain how another community of people use money.
2	Graphic organizer	Cameras and digital image repositories	Students will make a digital collage about natural resources that are abundant in their local area, ones that come from elsewhere, and ones that are scarce.
4	RAFT (Role, Audience, Format, Topic)	Digital video	Students will make videos from different perspectives of the same historical event, intended for different audiences. They will then compare the videos to generate an opinion about the historical event.

Practical Approaches to Digitally Supported Disciplinary Literacy in Social Studies

In this chapter, we will focus on the Core Disciplinary Practice of *Recognizing or Comprehending Multiple Types of Texts*. We present our thinking on this topic through a 5th-grade lesson in which students use multiple types of resources to describe colonial life in America through a multiperspective lens. Learning about a time period by way of understanding the lives of people during that time is a common thread across elementary grades, and when approached from a disciplinary angle, it provides a subfocus of considering multiple perspectives in learning about history and culture through various types of sources, including primary sources.

SAMPLE LESSON: COMPREHENDING MULTIPLE TYPES OF TEXTS TO BETTER UNDERSTAND U.S. COLONIAL LIFE IN 5TH GRADE

In this final sample lesson chapter, students will work to comprehend and illustrate the consistencies and inconsistencies across multiple perspectives of people who lived during the colonial time. The lesson varies somewhat from previous lesson examples as we decided to select a specific state's social studies standard to create a more targeted lesson. In considering this standard and objective, there is a logical connection to the Core Disciplinary Practice of *Recognizing or Comprehending Multiple Types of Text*. To most effectively compare perspectives, students will need to access and learn from a range of text types, including photographs, images, resource videos, firsthand journal accounts (in either print or audio format), historical ledgers, letters, and more, and this lesson illustrates how teachers might support students in this type of instruction.

Phase 1: Identifying Appropriate Disciplinary Literacy Practices

Table 10.1 represents the first phase of using the PEDDL Framework to support disciplinary literacy practices in social studies, which involves identifying the current standards guiding the lesson. This lesson is informed by a state standard, which is different from previous content lessons in this book, emphasizing the need for students to apply social science skills to understand how colonial life America was shaped. As shown in Table 10.1, by integrating the Core Disciplinary Practice of *Recognizing or Comprehending Multiple Types of Text* into the lesson, we also can address the following Common Core reading standard: "CCSS.ELA-Literacy.RI.3.7. Use information gained from illustrations (e.g., maps, photographs) and the words in a text to demonstrate understanding of the text (e.g., where, when, why, and how key events occur)." Important to elementary grades, this standard promotes the development of particular literacy skills that align with the social studies state standard. Finally, we used the C3 Framework for Social Studies Standards (NCSS, 2013) as a reference to confirm that we were promoting important disciplinary social studies skills for grade 5 learning. We use these three separate standards primarily for illustration to show the multiple ways in which understanding multiple sources of information is critical to learning in history and how this focus moves instruction beyond the more traditional approach of using a textbook as the primary source of information. We do not wish to downplay the importance of a textbook. Indeed, textbooks can provide a broad historical overview important to initial understandings of a time period. However, standards indicate textbooks should be supplemented with resources that provide a closer look at the different voices in history to gain a more balanced understanding of colonial life.

Phase 2: Framing Disciplinary Literacy

In Phase 2, consideration should be given to determining the essential information that students need to learn and why they need to understand the Core Disciplinary Practice related to this topic. Because both text recognition and comprehension are goals of instruction to support comparison and contrast between perspectives, two essential questions may be used and are noted in Table 10.1. In this lesson, students are exposed to learning from the kinds of texts that historians use to gain insight into people, places, and situations from the past. The ability to analyze and learn from multimodal sources of information such as photographs, drawings, paintings, records and notices, songs, and other documents is essential for historians and for supporting more-complex literacy skills useful for analysis and disciplinary comprehension. In 5th grade, it becomes increasingly important not only that students recognize the importance of studying different types of history texts, but that they know how to read across and understand those texts. These are complex skills, to be certain. Therefore, it is important to begin honing these skills in elementary grades. Further, different types of texts require different strategies for comprehending meaning and drawing conclusions. Thus, it is important that teachers provide instruction on strategies for comprehending different modes of text, which we also will highlight in Phase 5.

Table 10.1. Planning Outline

Current Instructional Considerations	Disciplinary Extensions
PHASE 1: Identifying Appropriate Disciplinary Literacy Practices	
What state/national standards am I targeting?	What Core Disciplinary Practices are supported by those standards and objectives?
Virginia Social Studies Standard of Learning USI.5.d. The student will apply social science skills to understand the factors that shaped colonial America by describing colonial life in America from the perspectives of large landowners, farmers, artisans, merchants, women, free African Americans, indentured servants, and enslaved African Americans.	Recognizing or comprehending multiple types of text
CCSS.ELA-Literacy.RI.3.7. Use information gained from illustrations (e.g., maps, photographs) and the words in a text to demonstrate understanding of the text (e.g., where, when, why, and how key events occur).	
C3 Framework for Social Studies Standards D2.His.10.3-5. Compare information provided by different historical sources about the past.	
What are my lesson objectives? After reading secondary sources, such as the textbook and historical fiction, students will be able to list multiple characteristics of colonial life in America.	
What are my revised lesson objectives? Students will use information from photographs, illustrations, and picture books to understand and illustrate the similarities and differences between different perspectives in a particular period in U.S. history.	

(table continues on next page)

Table 10.1. Planning Outline *(continued)*

Current Instructional Considerations	Disciplinary Extensions
PHASE 2: Framing Disciplinary Literacy	
What information is important for my students to learn and understand from this lesson? 1. Time and place, along with social stations, gender, and race, affect interpretations of history. 2. Information comes in many forms other than word-based text. Multiple types of texts and perspectives should be considered to more fully understand colonial life in America.	Why is it important for students to learn and understand this topic? Information comes in many forms, and perspective can influence the way in which we understand it. Historians consistently rely on multiple modes of information to gain insight on historical people and places. What essential question(s) might frame the importance of understanding this topic? 1. How does comparing perspectives on colonial life help us better understand the history of the United States? 2. Why is it important to use multiple types of texts when studying a specific point in history?
PHASE 3: Selecting Multimodal Texts for Disciplinary Literacy	
What texts does my school or school district require when teaching this topic? U.S. history textbook What texts do I feel comfortable using to support students' learning? Which topical texts align with my students' current reading levels? • Leveled readers • Picture books	What digital and multimodal texts might supplement my currently used texts and extend students' learning to encourage disciplinary literacy? • Websites containing primary source information in multiple formats (e.g., PBS) • Images and photographs • Records and notices How might these digital and multimodal texts help support students to engage in more advanced reading, writing, and communication practices? Primary sources, particularly historical sources, can contain archaic language, art that students are unfamiliar with, or even type print that is difficult to read. Digital texts can provide audio to read text aloud, annotations to understand different aspects of text, or video recordings of historians discussing a text.

Table 10.1. Planning Outline *(continued)*

Current Instructional Considerations	Disciplinary Extensions
PHASE 4: Assessing Disciplinary Literacy with a Variety of Tools	
What assessments do I currently use to determine students' learning and understanding of this topic?	How can I incorporate digital tools to further assess students' understanding of disciplinary practices and texts?
Text-based Venn diagram worksheet	In small groups, students can use a collaborative digital tool (e.g., Google Drawings) to create a group graphic organizer. Each student in a group can select from a teacher-created repository a text that appeals to them and use a "Questioning the Author" approach to examine and critique the text. Students can add their findings to the Google Drawing graphic organizer to create a cross-text comparison digital document. Google Drawings will enable students to add examples and evidence from multiple types of text (e.g., photos, screenshots, images, audio clips, videos, etc.) to create a comprehensive overview of multiple perspectives that they can then discuss as a group.
What type(s) of knowledge (e.g., fact-based, process-based, etc.) do those assessments gauge?	
Comparison and contrast of single-source facts	
	How do these digital tools create or support a more comprehensive assessment of students' understanding?
	Allowing students to select texts and tools that enable them to analyze and include a full range of textual examples helps support various types of learners and helps the teacher see how well students are able to understand and use information from a variety of text types.

(table continues on next page)

Table 10.1. Planning Outline *(continued)*

Current Instructional Considerations	Disciplinary Extensions
PHASE 5: Digitally Supporting Disciplinary Literacy Instruction	
How do I prepare my students to learn this topic? Have a class discussion, using the class textbook, on what students know about colonial life in America. **How do I guide my students' comprehension of this topic?** Assign picture-oriented books related to colonial life. Provide paper-based organizational charts with teacher-developed questions to answer regarding information read in texts. **How do I help my students reflect on their learning of this topic?** Discuss their responses as a class or in a small group.	**What digital tools extend and deepen students' preparation to learn this topic?** Provide students with access to the online Smithsonian Learning Lab (learninglab.si.edu). The teacher will model using this site and provide students guided practice in exploring the resources. **What digital tools can I incorporate to scaffold students' disciplinary comprehension?** Allow students to explore selected resources with a partner or in groups in the online Smithsonian Learning Lab. Students can choose to explore audio, video, or image collections to access information in a variety of formats that best align with their interests and abilities. Students will organize information learned in a digital Venn diagram. **What digital tools support and extend students' synthesis of learning of this topic?** Students audio-record their take-away ideas using the digital graphic organizer as a guide. Alternatively, students could audio-record a screencast explaining their graphic organizer. **What digital tools support students' development of artifacts to illustrate disciplinary literacy?** The audio recording will serve as the culminating artifact to represent students' learning from this lesson.

Table 10.1. Planning Outline (*continued*)

Current Instructional Considerations	Disciplinary Extensions
PHASE 6: Reflecting to Reach All Learners	
How have I differentiated instruction in this lesson? • Students can choose resources they want to study. • The collaborative digital graphic organizer provides students with numerous options for expression (images, audio, print-based text, etc.) and allows a variety of perspectives, based on multiple students' work, to be presented.	How have I considered personal, social, and cultural understandings that inform this lesson? Using the online Smithsonian Learning Lab provides students with multiple ways to engage with the content and many different representations of the content, and the digital graphic organizer provides multiple ways for students to express their understanding. Collectively, these options allow for differences in and provide support for personal, social, and cultural understandings.

Phase 3: Selecting Multimodal Texts for Disciplinary Literacy

As outlined in Table 10.1, we consider what texts often are required for teaching the content, as well as the variety of additional texts that will encourage learning of the Core Disciplinary Practice and support students in engaging in more advanced reading, writing, and communication practices. Social studies often relies on a textbook that summarizes historical information in a reader-friendly manner. This singular text can open up many opportunities for supplemental texts, but choosing supplemental texts also can seem overwhelming because of the infinite number of meaningful texts that can be used for instruction. Although it may be difficult to narrow the options, with the PEDDL Framework we recommend that teachers start with the materials they are most comfortable with and that align with students' reading levels. These texts likely will include leveled readers or other leveled text and picture-oriented books that are read as part of a whole-class read-aloud to ground an overall understanding of colonial life. Then, it is important to consider what digital and/or multimodal texts will support students in learning the specific disciplinary content and standards being addressed in the lesson.

In this case, students need to compare and consider multiple perspectives, including those of large landowners, farmers, artisans, merchants, women, free African Americans, indentured servants, and enslaved African Americans. This approach will require students to not only read books on the subject, but also review images, photographs, and audio/video-based information found on resource websites (PBS [www.pbs.org] and the Smithsonian Learning Lab [learninglab.si.edu/] are always great places to start) to gain a complete picture of colonial life, while addressing the target Core Disciplinary Practice.

Further, although searching for, locating, and evaluating information online are important digital literacy skills for 5th-graders, these are also complex skills to layer with a disciplinary approach to instruction at this level. Certainly, it will be important for students to have instruction in locating and evaluating online resources, but we suggest for this lesson that teachers find resources beforehand that represent a variety of perspectives in multiple formats. However, teachers may use this lesson as an opportunity to model online search skills while they locate resources as a whole-class activity or perhaps ask students to evaluate certain resources that have been curated by the teacher. This is all to say that digitally supported disciplinary literacy instruction places the primary focus on the Core Disciplinary Practice and seeks ways to effectively utilize digital tools to support literacy learning that may be too complex without digital aids.

Phase 4: Assessing Disciplinary Literacy with a Variety of Tools

Phase 4 of the PEDDL Framework guides us to consider how digital tools can provide unique opportunities for assessment and provide students with multiple ways to represent their disciplinary knowledge. In this lesson, students, as a group, review the information presented in many different formats, such as visual, audio, and text, supported by various digital features to aid in comprehension. Students are asked to select one text that they feel most comfortable working with and are provided a strategy to use (Questioning the Author) to analyze that source and document understandings.

As it can be difficult to fully represent information from an image or other digital resource in text form, it is unlikely that completing a paper-based graphic organizer will allow students to express the full range of ideas gained from the multiple text formats. Consequently, we recognize that using a digital tool, such as Google Drawings, to create a graphic organizer will better serve students in expressing their understanding. Using a digital tool enables students to insert images, audio files, and website links, and also include typed text. This gives students more expressive options for presenting facts and explaining their process for coming to their conclusions, since they will be able to include their resources in their final product. Finally, this tool is collaborative so students can digitally compile their shared learning into a document that then can be used to discuss colonial America from various perspectives.

Phase 5: Digitally Supporting Disciplinary Literacy Instruction

In Phase 5 we consider whether there are any digital tools that may help support or deepen students' comprehension of the content and prepare them for learning about the topic. Because this lesson engages students in exploring multiple perspectives in colonial American life, they are likely to be unfamiliar with all of the perspectives included. Students may benefit from having many visual examples related to the content in order to build their background knowledge before even beginning their work. Thus, here we suggest making use of resources such as the online Smithsonian Learning Lab, which provides an abundance of resources, including primary source materials and images of artifacts that can be examined alone or in collections. Although students would need instruction in how to locate and understand these materials because they will be exploring the materials independently, the use of a singular website may further scaffold elementary students in exploring multiple digital artifacts.

We note that, given the discrepancies between different classes' online experiences, the artifacts from the online Smithsonian Learning Lab could be used as part of whole-class instruction, as paired work, or independently, depending on search and comprehension skills needed to use this resource. Having students use the Questioning the Author strategy will contribute to the group's digital graphic organizer as they move through the Smithsonian Learning Lab, and will give students a digitally compatible resource to organize their online learning, along with print-based learning. In allowing students to audio-record their learning using the graphic organizer created by the group, the teacher enables students to bypass traditional writing, which may hinder some students in fully explaining their learning, particularly given the digital format of many of the resources studied. Further, assigning only one or two student-selected historical resources lowers the pressure for students who may feel less comfortable with this type of analysis, and provides students an opportunity to study resources most applicable to their interests or personal background.

Phase 6: Reflecting to Reach All Learners

Phase 6 of the PEDDL Framework encourages us to consider how students' individual interests, backgrounds, and needs are accounted for in the lesson. Specific needs will vary by classroom and lesson. In this lesson, we believe that student needs are accounted for because there are many options for how students can present their ideas in multiple formats, beyond word-based writing, in the digital graphic organizer, and they can choose which resources they want to study in a group jigsaw format. Additionally, the Smithsonian Learning Lab provides students with multiple ways to engage with the content, with many different representations of the content, and with multiple ways to express their understanding of the content. Collectively, these options allow for differences in and provide support for academic, personal, social, and cultural differences.

QUESTIONS TO PONDER

1. How do I support students in selecting a text to study/analyze?

We suggest when introducing the concept of the different types of texts historians use to study history that teachers do a type of "text talk" (think along the lines of a book talk) in which they discuss text features, along with the benefits and challenges that may accompany reading those texts. This type of talk need not be done with every lesson. Instead, consider incorporating it early in the year and provide refresher tips as needed. Or, engage in creating a word wall focused on different types of texts specific to each discipline for continued reference.

2. How do I feasibly support students in comprehending the text selected?

As we noted in this lesson, selecting one content literacy strategy for students to use regardless of text type is important in supporting comprehension. Try a strategy, like Questioning the Author, that provides students with general prompts or questions (e.g., What is the author trying to say?) to consider as they read/study to better understand the text.

3. What if students feel more comfortable using pencil and paper to hold their thoughts in a digital organizer as they study a text?

Let them use pencil and paper! If the technology overcomes or inhibits the lesson objective or goal, let students use a technique that they are comfortable with. Particularly, in this lesson students eventually will move their thoughts to the digital graphic organizer to collaborate with others. Although this transition would be smoother going from digital platform to digital platform, we recognize that some students need more practice using digital tools. We encourage teachers to allow opportunities in other areas of instruction for students to use digital organizers, as many students find these tools more accessible because they often require a lower level of traditional writing skills. With practice, students will develop confidence in using these tools.

4. How do I support students who have never used a collaborative digital graphic organizer?

Provide low-risk, nondisciplinary opportunities for students to play in these digital environments. Have students do a quick practice in organizing information in a nonacademic text, such as a cartoon or short video. Additionally, we ask teachers to keep in mind the multiple demands of the disciplinary literacy skills required for this lesson. However, if teachers decide to engage students in locating and evaluating online information, a great resource for learning more about teaching students to locate and evaluate online resources is the book *Reading the Web* (Dobler & Eagleton, 2015).

To expand on our examples of integrating digitally supported disciplinary literacy in social studies, we also provide in online Appendix D a completed kindergarten lesson plan, using the PEDDL Lesson Plan Template. In that lesson plan, we outline how a teacher might plan an original lesson for kindergarten students to demonstrate skills for historical thinking by sequencing events from the past that show how their community has changed over time. The plan incorporates the book *The House on Maple Street* by Bonnie Pryor (1992), along with a guest speaker who will incorporate the same Core Disciplinary Practice of focus as in this lesson (*Recognizing or Comprehending Multiple Types of Text*) by sharing photographs of the history of the community in which the students live. In doing so, we are able to provide a comparison of how this Core Disciplinary Practice might look in different elementary grade levels.

CHAPTER 11

Closing Thoughts and Tips for Planning

As Ms. Branch begins planning her next units, she plans to use the PEDDL Framework to inform the standards she selects, and most important, the way she interprets those standards as learning objectives for her students. She will continue to draw on the 3rd-grade expectations in her building and district, but will focus on privileging disciplinary knowledge alongside content knowledge and considering digital tools to support students' learning of both types of knowledge. In some cases, she will find that she uses the PEDDL Framework to substantially revise the instruction to draw on digital texts and tools to allow students to explore new cultural understandings beyond what her traditional instruction may allow. In others, she may find that small adjustments to highlight the disciplinary literacies involved in content standards appropriately meet students' learning needs. She knows that this will be a learning process and that, just as when she introduces any new material, she may have to adjust her planning. However, she feels that her students will be better prepared for the traditional and digital realities of learning in English, math, science, and social studies.

We hope that our teacher readers, just as Ms. Branch, continue to process and consider digitally supported disciplinary literacy as they move forward in future planning. Indeed, this book provides considerable information about how to plan for digitally supported disciplinary literacy. And, as we reread the sum of this text we have written, we fully recognize the daunting task of considering and integrating disciplinary literacy and digital tools into K–5 instruction. But our work in teacher education has proven time and time again that teachers are up to the challenge! Accordingly, we close this book with brief final considerations to keep in mind as you begin the process of, or initial thinking about, your instructional planning for digitally supported disciplinary literacy.

LONG-RANGE PLANNING

Long-range plans related to the intentional integration of digital tools have been shown to support teachers in effectively integrating technology

(Beschorner & Woodward, 2019), and other long-range plans around curriculum mapping and materials frequently are used in grade-level instructional planning. While formal long-range plans specifically focused on digitally supported disciplinary literacy are not necessary, we do suggest a critical evaluation of existing long-range plans to look for points in curricula where this type of instruction naturally might fit. For example, where might the Core Disciplinary Practices described in this text further benefit your students' learning and extend learning goals or objectives to enhance real-world or life/personal connections? Perhaps add a column to your current long-range plans to make those connections. These practices need not fit in each unit, but providing students with instruction and experiences once a month or a few times a quarter, when relevant, may enhance their literacy learning and better prepare them for disciplinary instruction in the upper grades.

Tables 11.1 and 11.2 provide an example of a long-range plan with possible disciplinary extensions and digital tools to support students in learning the Core Disciplinary Practices. In this table there are several things of note that may assist you in considering how to integrate disciplinary literacy learning into your everyday instruction. First, you can see that the plan extends the same Core Disciplinary Practice over multiple topics and weeks. If the same Core Disciplinary Practice can logically connect to the skills or standards taught in consecutive weeks, it makes sense to focus on the same Core Disciplinary Practice for multiple standards. This approach may provide opportunities to deepen understanding of the Core Disciplinary Practice, and also may decrease the amount of time that needs to be spent on developing the practice in a given week.

In Table 11.1 you also will see that the plan does not include Core Disciplinary Practices every week. It may make sense to not incorporate a Core Disciplinary Practice every week if there is no seemingly logical connection between the topic or standard and the Core Disciplinary Practices or there are other instructional priorities that may prevent this integration. Further, in Table 11.2 there are ideas for possible digital tools for supporting students in learning the content and the Core Disciplinary Practices. These ideas are preliminary and must be re-evaluated when the teacher actually plans the lessons with the PEDDL Framework. However, adding digital tool suggestions to the long-range plan can help teachers to see the variety of digital tools that they integrate, and to consider whether students have the digital skills they need in order to use these tools and how to support them in developing those skills. Finally, you will see that below the table there is a list of the types of digital tools that may support and enhance student learning. This list is there simply as a tool for teachers to use as they plan. Having such a list can help you consider the range of tools that may be used to enhance learning of the Core Disciplinary Practices.

Table 11.1. Sample Long-Range Plan with Disciplinary Extensions

Topic or Standard	Time Frame	Possible Disciplinary Extensions
Students will: • Collect numerical data and record, organize, display, and interpret the data.	September 2 weeks	**Core Disciplinary Practice:** Developing and communicating ideas, arguments, or rationalizations **Possible Digital Tools:** Use the Explain Everything app for students to photograph their number sentences, bar graphs, or picture graphs and explain their meaning.
Students will: • Count, read, and write whole numbers to 1,000. • Identify the place value of each digit.	September 1 week	**Core Disciplinary Practice:** Developing and communicating ideas, arguments, or rationalizations **Possible Digital Tools:** Use a digital tool such as Flipgrid for students to record and share their understanding of place value, regrouping, and different ways to make numbers.
Students will: • Order and compare whole numbers to 1,000 by using symbols.	September 1 week	**Core Disciplinary Practice:** None
Students will: • Demonstrate an understanding of patterns and how patterns grow, and describe them in general ways.	October 2 weeks	**Core Disciplinary Practice:** Analysis across multiple texts **Possible Digital Tools:** Use ScratchJr to animate a pattern that students create or find in nature.
Students will: • Solve problems using combinations of coins and bills.	October 2 weeks	**Core Disciplinary Practices:** 1. Developing and communicating ideas, arguments, or rationalizations 2. Analysis across multiple texts **Possible Digital Tools:** Students video-record explanations of the solution to a problem. Students watch videos of other students' solutions and look for patterns in how students solved the problem.

Table 11.2. Digital Tool Types to Consider Incorporating

• Audio-recording tools	• Drawing tools
• Collaborative-writing tools	• Video creation tools
• Digital presentation tools	• Digital books
• Tools for sharing digital creations	• Text annotation tools
	• Screencasting tools
• Coding tools	• Digital graphic organizers
• Digital video sites	

TIME, TIME, TIME

Related to long-range planning, the most common reaction we receive when introducing digitally supported disciplinary literacy instruction to teachers is that although they appreciate this type of instruction, they do not have time to "add" anything else to what they currently teach. We completely understand this concern in present-day education, where teachers are being asked to do more with fewer resources and less time. Yet, the teachers with whom we have worked noted that, as they gain practice with using the PEDDL Framework, they understand that disciplinary literacy is not a wildly different instructional approach and, more often than not, aligns with broad instructional goals, often requiring minor tweaks rather than major reworking of instruction. Also, many teachers currently are looking for meaningful ways to incorporate technology into their classrooms. These revelations somewhat alleviate concerns about the amount of time it may take to use this type of instruction.

As with any shift in instructional planning, it is important to establish reasonable expectations and manageable goals. For example, many of the lessons discussed throughout the chapters of this book use existing materials, standards, and objectives as the foundation for instruction, rather than starting completely from scratch. Focusing on unpacking the standards for an upcoming unit may be a useful first step to fully integrating digital disciplinary literacy into instruction.

This approach is also useful when selecting new digital tools and disciplinary literacy concepts to support student learning. By building on the digital skills that students already have and using those skills as a springboard to intentionally integrate more-complex digital tools, teachers better prepare students for success (Hutchison & Colwell, 2016). The same idea is useful when introducing new disciplinary literacy concepts, as utilizing digital tools that students are already familiar with or that are particularly intuitive can allow students to foreground the new disciplinary literacy learning. Intentionally scaffolding the introduction of new digital tools and disciplinary literacy concepts may make the process of integrating digitally supported disciplinary literacy into existing instruction easier.

DESIGNING INSTRUCTION
THAT IS APPROPRIATE FOR ALL STUDENTS

Although it is possible that integrating digital tools into instruction may increase the length of lessons, it is also possible that integrating digital tools and planning with the PEDDL Framework can save time by providing ways to simultaneously support a range of abilities, preferences, and cultural backgrounds among students. Throughout this book we have touched on the importance of planning instruction that is inclusive and encompassing of all students, and is designed to highlight the strengths of all students. Planning with the PEDDL Framework and integrating digital tools helps teachers to explicitly consider and address the cultural and academic backgrounds and intellectual and social needs of students.

As we have argued before, a disciplinary literacy approach to planning instruction offers built-in opportunities to deliberately connect to students' cultural backgrounds and intellectual differences. Disciplinary literacy instruction should employ a wide variety of texts, which increases opportunities for students to come into contact with perspectives and cultural viewpoints similar to their own, especially when a wide variety of digital texts are integrated into instruction. Also, disciplinary literacy focuses on addressing real-world issues, which may be more relevant and engaging for all students as they connect school to life. All of this adds up to creating a classroom environment in which students are prepared to learn and willing and able to do so because of the relevant and appropriate instruction that has been prepared for them. Using the PEDDL Framework to plan instruction can save time by giving teachers an approach for proactively addressing all of these considerations.

INTRODUCING NEW DIGITAL TOOLS TO STUDENTS

Considerations of time bring us to ideas related specifically to using and introducing new digital tools in instruction. In elementary grades, especially, there can be a learning curve in successful digital tool use as young students may not have much or any experience using digital tools. Accordingly, here we offer suggestions for selecting tools that are relevant, useful, and developmentally appropriate.

First, it is essential that teachers select appropriate tools that are well-aligned with the intended instructional outcomes. The PEDDL Framework helps ensure that the intended use of the digital tool is closely aligned with

the instructional objectives, and that the tool is used in a way that supports
the development of disciplinary literacy skills, and supports and enhances
students' learning experiences. Still, once the type of tool is chosen (e.g., a
digital graphic organizer), the teacher must consider carefully the specific
tool that will be used. For example, a teacher wishing to incorporate a digital graphic organizer tool will have an abundance of options from which to
choose. Thus, we recommend that teachers do the following:

1. Narrow the list by looking for a tool that has all of the specific
   features needed. This will quickly help teachers go from an
   abundance of choices to just a few.
2. Try out the tool by mimicking what students will do with the tool.
   Consider how simple it is to use, how easy it is to navigate, and
   whether there are distracting content features.
3. Consider students' current digital skills. Do they have previous
   experience using this kind of tool? Does it require a sign-in that
   could be problematic for students? Can students quickly learn to
   navigate the tool or will it require extensive instruction?
4. Consider the intended purpose for using the digital tool. Is this
   particular digital tool well-aligned with that purpose? If the digital
   tool will be used to create a product, consider whether the tool will
   help students easily create the intended product.

DISCREPANCIES ACROSS GRADES K-5

Aside from the multiple-discipline instruction required of elementary teachers, perhaps the most difficult part of disciplinary literacy instruction, and
one that we have attempted to address in the lesson plan examples, is in the
reality that the literacy abilities of a kindergarten student are vastly different than those of a 5th-grader. The majority of kindergarten students begin
compulsory education not knowing how to read or write, and finish 5th
grade reading and writing a variety of formats, topics, and styles. Certainly,
5th-grade instruction much more closely mirrors middle school education,
where content is a priority and the disciplines are clearly defined. Thus, it
may seem inherently less difficult to plan for digitally supported disciplinary
literacy in upper elementary grades than lower grades. However, our disciplinary practice chapters highlight goals and discipline-friendly methods
that are suited to the range of elementary grades.

The goal of our lesson plan chapters and the examples in our online
Appendices A–D is to show that as students gain more domain knowledge
about each of the disciplines, they are better prepared to engage in increasingly complex disciplinary literacy knowledge. For example, consider the
four Core Disciplinary Practices discussed throughout this book:

1. Recognizing and comprehending multiple text types
2. Analyzing text
3. Using vocabulary particular to a discipline
4. Communicating an argument, rationalization, or understanding

As younger students engage in *recognizing and comprehending multiple text types*, much of this learning is focused on differences between fiction and nonfiction, and the existence of multiple forms of text. As students build an understanding of these ideas, their disciplinary literacy knowledge of multiple texts should grow as well and instruction should become more explicit.

While much of early literacy learning and disciplinary analysis of text is focused on main ideas and summaries, these skills serve as an important and necessary foundation to support students' ability to *analyze text*. Older students who are learning specific disciplinary terms and how to *use vocabulary particular to a discipline* rely on word attack strategies and an understanding, established in earlier grades, that different disciplines use different words. Finally, students who are learning how to write gain disciplinary knowledge as they draw and label pictures, write personal narratives, and write or record descriptions of natural phenomena, which serve as the groundwork for more sophisticated ways of *communicating an argument, rationalization, or understanding*. While digitally supported disciplinary literacy instruction is critical at each grade, it also must be integrated differently at each grade, representing a continuum of disciplinary literacy from kindergarten to 5th grade.

EXPLICIT DISCIPLINARY LITERACY INSTRUCTION

This consideration could cross-cut K–12 instruction, but particularly we highlight that any disciplinary literacy instruction incorporated into elementary grades should be made explicit to students. Just as important as helping students gain experience with disciplinary literacy in K–5 is that they are aware that they are engaging in disciplinary literacy. Further, in these grades, where disciplinary literacy practices may need to be modified to be grade-level appropriate, it is important for students to be aware of how they are learning about disciplinary literacy.

Certainly, it is well known that explicit instruction is critical to literacy instruction. Not only did the National Reading Panel (2000) support explicit instruction related to all five components of effective literacy instruction, but explicit instruction continues to be relevant in the areas of culturally responsive pedagogy (Naraian, 2016), digital literacy (Kang, 2018), supporting English language learners (Bauer & Arazi, 2011), and disciplinary instruction such as science (McTigue & Flowers, 2011).

The benefits of explicit instruction extend to instruction related to disciplinary literacy. The need for explicit instruction related to disciplinary literacy has been noted in the body of disciplinary literacy research in secondary schools (Fang & Schleppegrell, 2010; Shanahan & Shanahan, 2008) as a response to the opaque nature of disciplinary literacy in the upper grades. Through integrating disciplinary literacy instruction and recognizing disciplinary texts in elementary grades, teachers enable students to acquire the domain knowledge needed to understand the complex, and sometimes nuanced, disciplinary practices they are expected to come to secondary school already knowing.

ESTABLISHING A PROFESSIONAL LEARNING NETWORK

Much of our research with teachers has focused on how professional learning networks (PLNs) may support teachers in taking on disciplinary literacy instruction (Colwell & Hutchison, 2018; Colwell & Taylor, 2019), successfully using new approaches in learning (Popp & Goldman, 2016), and using digital tools to promote learning (Hutchison & Woodward, 2018).

Our findings from this body of work suggest that establishing a digital or face-to-face PLN of similar grade-level teachers, within either a building, school division, or state, may positively aid teachers in digitally supported disciplinary literacy instruction. The same hallmarks of a PLN that work to support other approaches to instruction can be readily leveraged to assist teachers as they integrate new digital tools, existing digital tools in new ways, and disciplinary literacy concepts. Through co-planning, identifying approaches to overcoming barriers, and exploring research-supported instructional practices, teachers can plan collaboratively to support disciplinary learning alongside existing instructional goals.

Additionally, we suggest that teachers consider including disciplinary experts as part of PLNs. Throughout the book, we have sought to situate elementary students' understanding of disciplinary practices in ways that resonate with real-world applications of what experts in each field do professionally. Strengthening teachers' understanding of the disciplinary literacies and digital tools experts use can facilitate identifying disciplinary practices within elementary standards. Not only can digital tools support students' learning about disciplinary literacy, but there are a number of digital methods that can connect teachers to experts for their own professional learning. Whether it involves video lectures or examples, viewing published artifacts or work, or actually connecting with local experts through video chats with a class, there are a number of ways to utilize connections with experts to inform your own digitally supported disciplinary literacy planning.

We have found that one of the best ways to connect with disciplinary experts is through social media. Many experts are active on social media, sharing resources and sometimes hosting Twitter chats. Additionally, many professional organizations have active social media accounts through which they share resources, links to new research, and more. We recommend seeking out experts and professional organizations through social media as one way to begin developing your professional learning network.

FINAL REMARKS

In conclusion, we express our thanks for the time spent reading and considering the content of this book. We hope it inspires and prompts action in digitally supported disciplinary literacy instruction. As we wrote in the very first sentence of the Introduction, we once again note that we, the authors, are not digital natives and we did not learn about disciplinary literacy instruction for elementary students in our teacher education programs. Rather, all of us have come to value the powerful ways that digital technology can support the teaching and development of reading, writing, and communication skills in the academic disciplines. We hope that this text illustrates the value of this approach and supports planning that provides students a strong foundation for disciplinary literacy that leads to success in upper grades and in life.

References

Altieri, J. L. (2011). *Content counts! Developing disciplinary literacy skills, K–6.* Newark, DE: International Reading Association.

Alvermann, D. E., Gillis, V. R., & Phelps, S. F. (2012). *Content area reading and literacy: Succeeding in today's diverse classroom* (7th ed.). Boston, MA: Pearson.

Alvermann, D., & Wilson, A. (2011). Comprehension strategy instruction for multimodal texts in science. *Theory into Practice, 50,* 116–124. doi:10.1080/0040 5841.2011.558436

Artell, M. (2001). *Petite Rouge: A Cajun Red Riding Hood.* New York, NY: Puffin Books.

Bauer, E. B., & Arazi, J. (2011). Promoting literacy development for beginning English learners. *The Reading Teacher, 64*(5), 383–386.

Bean, T. W. (2000). Reading in the content areas: Social constructivist dimensions. In M. L. Kamil, P. B. Mosenthal, P. D. Pearson, & R. Barr (Eds.), *Handbook of reading research* (Vol. 3, pp. 629–654). Mahwah, NJ: Erlbaum.

Beck, I. L., McKeown, M. G., Hamilton, R. L., & Kucan, L. (1997). *Questioning the Author: An approach for enhancing student engagement with text.* Newark, DE: International Reading Association.

Beck, I. L., McKeown, M. G., Sinatra, G. M., & Loxterman, J. A. (1991). Revising social studies text from a text-processing perspective: Evidence of improved comprehensibility. *Reading Research Quarterly, 26*(3), 251–276.

Beschorner, B., & Woodward, L. (2019). Long term planning for technology in literacy instruction. *The Reading Teacher, 73*(3), 325–337. https://doi.org/10.1002/trtr.1828

Britt, J., & Ming, K. (2017). Applying disciplinary literacy in elementary geography. *Geography Teacher, 14*(2), 68–76.

Brock, C. H., Goatley, V. J., Raphael, T. E., Trost-Shahata, E., & Weber, C. M. (2014). *Engaging students in disciplinary literacy, K–6.* New York, NY: Teachers College Press.

Caparo, R. M., Caparo, M. M., & Rupley, W. H. (2010). Semantics and syntax: A theoretical model for how students may build mathematical misunderstandings. *Journal of Mathematics Education, 3*(2), 58–66.

Cappello, M., & Lafferty, K. (2015). The roles of photography for developing literacy across the disciplines. *Reading Teacher, 69*(3), 287–295.

Castek, J., & Manderino, M. (2017). A planning framework for integrating digital literacies for disciplinary learning. *Journal of Adolescent & Adult Literacy, 60*(6), 697–700.

Center for Applied Special Technology. (2019). About universal design for learning. Retrieved from www.cast.org/our-work/about-udl.html#.XL81e_ZKhBx

Colwell, J. (2019). Selecting texts for disciplinary literacy instruction. *The Reading Teacher, 72*(5), 631–637. doi:10.1002/trtr.1762

Colwell, J., & Hutchison, A. C. (2015). Refining a flipped classroom model in a content area literacy course: Determining modification through reflection. *International Journal of Social Media and Interactive Learning Environments*, 3(4), 249–266.

Colwell, J., & Hutchison, A. C. (2018). Considering a Twitter-based professional learning network in literacy education. *Literacy Research & Instruction*, 57(1), 5–25.

Colwell, J., & Taylor, V. (2019). Peer review in online professional communities to support elementary disciplinary literacy planning. In R. Karchmer-Klein & K. Pytash (Eds.), *Effective practices in online teacher preparation for literacy educators* (pp. 107–127). Hershey, PA: IGI Global.

Common Core State Standards Initiative. (2019). Standards for mathematical practice. Retrieved from www.corestandards.org/Math/Practice/

Dalton, B. (2012). Multimodal composition and the Common Core State Standards. *The Reading Teacher*, 66(4), 333–339.

De Lange, J. (2003). Mathematics for literacy. In M. Niss (Ed.), *Quantitative literacy and mathematical competencies* (pp. 75–89). Princeton, NJ: National Council on Education and the Disciplines.

Dobler, E., & Eagleton, M. (2015). *Reading the web*. New York, NY: Guilford Press.

Draper, R. J. (2002). Every teacher a literacy teacher? An analysis of the literacy-related messages in secondary methods textbooks. *Journal of Literacy Research*, 34(3), 357–384.

Draper, R. J., & Adair, M. (2010). (Re)Imagining literacies for science classrooms. In R. J. Draper (Ed.), & P. Broomhead, A. P. Jensen, J. D. Nokes, & D. Siebert (Co-Eds.), *(Re)Imagining content-area literacy instruction* (pp. 127–143). New York, NY: Teachers College Press.

Draper, R. J., Broomhead, P., Jensen, A. P., & Siebert, D. (2010). Aims and criteria for collaboration in content-area classrooms. In R. J. Draper (Ed.), & P. Broomhead, A. P. Jensen, J. D. Nokes, & D. Siebert (Co-Eds.), *(Re)Imagining content-area literacy instruction* (pp. 1–19). New York, NY: Teachers College Press.

Draper, R. J., & Siebert, D. (2010). Rethinking texts, literacies, and literacy across the curriculum. In R. J. Draper (Ed.), & P. Broomhead, A. P., Jensen, J. D. Nokes, & D. Siebert (Co-Eds.), *(Re)Imagining content-area literacy instruction* (pp. 20–39). New York, NY: Teachers College Press.

Duke, N. K. (2000). 3.6 minutes per day: The scarcity of informational texts in first grade. *Reading Research Quarterly*, 35, 202–224. dx.doi.org/10.1598/RRQ.35.2.1

Duke, N. K. (2010). The real-world reading and writing U.S. children need. *Phi Delta Kappan*, 91, 68–71. dx.doi.org/10.1177/003172171009100517

Dunkerly-Bean, J., & Bean, T. W. (2016). Missing the savoir for the connaissance: Disciplinary literacy and content area literacy as regimes of truth. *Journal of Literacy Research*, 48, 448–475.

Faggella-Luby, M. N., Graner, P. S., Deshler, D. D., & Drew, S. V. (2012). Building a house on sand: Why disciplinary literacy is not sufficient to replace general strategies for adolescent learners who struggle. *Topics in Language Disorders*, 32(1), 69–84.

Fang, Z., & Schleppegrell, M. J. (2010). Disciplinary literacies across content areas: Supporting secondary reading through functional language analysis. *Journal of Adolescent & Adult Literacy*, 53(7), 587–597.

Fisher, D., & Frey, N. (2012). Close reading in elementary schools. *The Reading Teacher, 66*(3), 179–188.

Fisher, R. (2019). Reconciling disciplinary literacy perspectives with genre-oriented activity theory: Toward a fuller synthesis of traditions. *Reading Research Quarterly, 54*(2), 237–251.

Frambaugh-Kritzer, C., Buelow, S., & Steele, J. S. (2015). What are disciplinary literacies in dance and drama in the elementary grades? *Journal of Language & Literacy Education, 11*(1), 65–87.

Gillis, V. (2014). Discipline literacy: Adapt, not adopt. *Journal of Adolescent & Adult Literacy, 57*(8), 614–623.

Håland, A. (2017). Disciplinary literacy in elementary school: How a struggling student positions herself as a writer. *The Reading Teacher, 70*(4), 457–468.

Halladay, J. L. & Neumann, M. D. (2012). Connecting reading and mathematical strategies. *The Reading Teacher, 65*(7), 471–476.

Hedin, L. R., & Conderman, G. (2010). Teaching students to comprehend informational texts through rereading. *The Reading Teacher, 63*(7), 556–565.

Herczog, M. M. (2010). The links between the C3 framework and the NCSS National Curriculum Standards for Social Studies. *Social Education, 77*(6), 331–333.

Hutchison, A. (2018). Using virtual reality to explore science and literacy concepts. *The Reading Teacher.* doi:10.1002/trtr.1720

Hutchison, A., & Beschorner, B. (2014). Using the iPad as a tool to support literacy instruction. *Technology, Pedagogy & Education, 24*(5), 407–422. doi:10.1080/1475939X.2014.918561

Hutchison, A., Beschorner, B., & Schmidt-Crawford, D. (2012). Exploring the use of the iPad for literacy learning. *The Reading Teacher, 66*(1), 15–23.

Hutchison, A., & Colwell, J. (2014). The potential of digital technologies to support literacy instruction relevant to the Common Core State Standards. *Journal of Adolescent & Adult Literacy, 58*(2), 147–156. doi:10.1002/jaal.335

Hutchison, A., & Colwell, J. (2015). *Bridging technology and literacy: Developing digital reading and writing practices in grades K–6.* Lanham, MD: Rowman & Littlefield.

Hutchison, A., & Colwell, J. (2016). Preservice teachers' use of the technology integration planning cycle to integrate iPads into literacy instruction. *Journal of Research on Technology in Education, 48*(1), 1–15.

Hutchison, A., Nadolny, L., & Estapa, A. (2016). Using coding apps to support literacy instruction and develop coding literacy. *The Reading Teacher, 69*(5), 493–503. doi:10.1002/trtr.1440

Hutchison, A., & Reinking, D. (2011). Teachers' perceptions of integrating information and communication technologies into literacy instruction: A national survey in the United States. *Reading Research Quarterly, 46*(4), 312–333.

Hutchison, A., & Woodward, L. (2014a). An examination of how a teacher's use of digital tools empowers and constrains language arts instruction. *Computers in the Schools, 31*(4), 316–338. doi:10.1080/07380569.2014.967629

Hutchison, A., & Woodward, L. (2014b). A planning cycle for integrating technology into literacy instruction. *The Reading Teacher, 67*(6), 455–464. doi:10.1002/trtr.1225

Hutchison, A., & Woodward, L. (2018). Examining the technology integration planning cycle model of professional development to support teachers' instructional practices. *Teachers College Record, 120*(10), 1–44.

Hutchison, A. C., Woodward, L., & Colwell, J. (2016). What are preadolescent readers doing online? An examination of upper elementary students' reading, writing, and communication in digital spaces. *Reading Research Quarterly, 51*(4), 361–477.

Hynd-Shanahan, C. (2013). What does it take? The challenge of disciplinary literacy. *Journal of Adolescent & Adult Literacy, 57*(2), 93–98.

International Literacy Association & National Council of Teachers of English. (2012). *Standards for the English language arts.* Newark, DE: Author. (Original work published 1996)

Juel, C., Hebard, H., Haubner, J. P., & Moran, M. (2010). Reading through a disciplinary lens. *Educational Leadership, 67*(6), 12–17.

Kang, G. Y. (2018). Playing with digital tools with explicit scaffolding. *The Reading Teacher, 71*(6), 735–741.

Ladson-Billings, G. (2014). Culturally relevant pedagogy 2.0: a.k.a. the remix. *Harvard Educational Review, 84*(1), 74–84.

Leedy, L. (1997). *Mission: Addition.* New York, NY: Holiday House.

Lemke, J. L. (2004). The literacies of science. In W. Saul (Ed.), *Crossing borders in literacy and science instruction: Perspectives on theory and practice* (pp. 33–47). Newark, DE: International Reading Association & National Science Teachers Association.

Lemley, S. M., Hart, S. M., & King, J. R. (2019). Teacher inquiry develops elementary teachers' disciplinary literacy. *Literacy Research and Instruction, 58*(1), 12–30.

Liebfreund, M. D., & Conradi, K. (2016). Component skills affecting elementary students' informational text comprehension. *Reading and Writing: An Interdisciplinary Journal, 29*(6), 1141–1160.

Luke, A., & Freebody, P. (1999). A map of possible practices: Further notes on the four resources model. *Practically Primary, 4*(2), 5–8.

Maloch, B., & Horsey, M. (2013). Living inquiry: Learning from and about informational texts in a second-grade classroom. *The Reading Teacher, 66*(6), 475–485.

Manderino, M., & Castek, J. (2016). Digital literacies for disciplinary learning: A call to action. *Journal of Adolescent & Adult Literacy, 60*(1), 79–81.

Marinak, B., & Gambrell, L. (2008). Elementary informational text instruction: A research review. *The International Journal of Learning: Annual Review, 15*(9), 75–84.

McTigue, E. M., & Flowers, A. C. (2011). Science visual literacy: Learners' perceptions and knowledge of diagrams: Diagrams found in science texts can be complex repositories of meaning, and students benefit from instruction in how to unlock them. *The Reading Teacher, 64*(8), 578–589.

Merkley, D. (1996/1997). Modified anticipation guide. *The Reading Teacher, 50*, 365–368.

Moje, E. B. (2008). Foregrounding the disciplines in secondary literacy teaching and learning: A call for change. *Journal of Adolescent & Adult Literacy, 52*(2), 96–107.

Moje, E. B. (2015). Doing and teaching disciplinary literacy with adolescent learners: A social and cultural enterprise. *Harvard Educational Review, 85*(2), 254–278.

Moll, L. C., Amanti, C., Neff, D., & Gonzalez, N. (1992). Funds of knowledge for teaching: Using a qualitative approach to connect homes and classrooms. *Theory into Practice, 31*(2), 132–141.

Moore, D. W., Readence, J. E., & Rickelman, R. J. (1983). An historical exploration of content area reading instruction. *Reading Research Quarterly, 18*, 419–483.

Naraian, S. (2016). Teaching for "real": Reconciling explicit literacy instruction with inclusive pedagogy in a fourth-grade urban classroom. *Urban Education, 54*(10), 1581–1607.

National Center for Education Statistics. (2018a, April). *Children and youth with disabilities.* Washington, DC: Institute of Education Sciences. Retrieved from nces.ed.gov/programs/coe/indicator_cgg.asp

National Center for Education Statistics. (2018b). *Digest of education statistics: 2016.* Washington, DC: Institute of Education Sciences. Retrieved from nces. ed.gov/programs/digest/d16/

National Council of Teachers of Mathematics. (2000). *Principles and standards for school mathematics.* Reston, VA: Author.

National Council of Teachers of Mathematics. (2013). *Principles to actions: An urgent agenda for school mathematics.* Reston, VA: Author.

National Council for the Social Studies. (2013). *The college, career, and civic life (C3) framework for the social studies state standards: Guidance for enhancing the rigor of K–12 civics, economics, geography, and history.* Silver Springs, MD: Author.

National Governors Association Center for Best Practices & Council of Chief State School Officers. (2010). *Common Core State Standards.* Washington, DC: Authors.

National Reading Panel. (2000). *Report of the National Reading Panel—Teaching children to read: An evidence-based assessment of the scientific research literature on reading and its implications for reading instruction.* Washington, DC: National Institute of Child Health and Human Development.

Next Generation Science Standards Lead States. (2013). *Next generation science standards: For states, by states.* Washington, DC: The National Academies Press.

Nokes, J. D. (2010). (Re)Imagining literacies for history classrooms. In R. J. Draper (Ed.), & P. Broomhead, A. P. Jensen, J. D. Nokes, & D. Siebert (Co-Eds.), *(Re) Imagining content-area literacy instruction* (pp. 54–68). New York, NY: Teachers College Press.

Ogle, D. M. (1986). K-W-L: A teaching model that develops active reading of expository text. *The Reading Teacher, 39*(6), 564–570.

Parenti, M. (2018). Becoming disciplined about disciplinary literacy through guided retelling. *The Reading Teacher, 71*(4), 473–478.

Peck, S. (2010). Not on the same page but working together: Lessons from an award-winning urban elementary school. *The Reading Teacher, 63*(5), 394–403.

Pennington, J. L., Obenchain, K. M., & Brock, C. H. (2014). Reading informational texts: A civic transactional perspective. *The Reading Teacher, 67*(7), 532–542.

Popp, J., & Goldman, S. (2016). Knowledge building in teacher professional learning communities: Focus of meeting matters. *Teaching and Teacher Education, 59*, 347–359.

Pryor, B. (1992). *The house on maple street.* New York, NY: HarperCollins.

Rainey, E. C. (2016). Disciplinary literacy in English language arts: Exploring the social and problem-based nature of literary reading and reasoning. *Reading Research Quarterly, 52*(1), 53–71.

Richardson, J. S., Morgan, R. F., & Fleener, C. E. (2012). *Reading to learn in the content areas: What's new in education* (8th ed.). Belmont, CA: Wadsworth.

Scieszka, J., & Smith, L. (1996). *The true story of the three little pigs*. New York, NY: Puffin Books.

Shanahan, C., & Shanahan, T. (2014). Does disciplinary literacy have a place in elementary school? *The Reading Teacher, 67*(8), 636–639.

Shanahan, T., & Shanahan, C. (2008). Teaching disciplinary literacy to adolescents: Rethinking content-area literacy. *Harvard Educational Review, 78*(1), 40–61.

Shanahan, T., & Shanahan, C. (2012). What is disciplinary literacy and why does it matter? *Topics in Language Disorders, 32*(1), 7–18.

Siebert, D., & Draper, R. J. (2012). Reconceptualizing literacy and instruction for mathematics classrooms. In T. L Jetton & C. Shanahan (Eds.), *Adolescent literacy in the academic disciplines* (pp. 172–198). New York, NY: Guilford Press.

Siffrinn, N., & Lew, S. (2018). Building disciplinary language and literacy in elementary teacher training. *The Reading Teacher, 72*(3), 325–341.

Smagorinsky, P. (2015). Disciplinary literacy in English language arts. *Journal of Adolescent & Adult Literacy, 59*(2), 141–146.

Spires, H. A., Kerkhoff, S. N., & Graham, A.C.K. (2016). Disciplinary literacy and inquiry: Teaching for deeper content learning. *Journal of Adolescent & Adult Literacy, 60*(2), 151–161.

Taie, S., & Goldring, R. (2017). *Characteristics of public elementary and secondary school teachers in the United States: Results from the 2015–16 National Teacher and Principal Survey*. Washington, DC: Institute of Education Sciences. Retrieved from nces.ed.gov/pubs2017/2017071.pdf

Thoma, J., Hutchison, A., Johnson, D., Johnson, K., & Stromer, E. (2017). Planning for technology integration in a professional learning community. *The Reading Teacher, 71*(2), 167–175. doi.org/10.1002/trtr.1604

Toppel, K. (2015). Enhancing core reading programs with culturally responsive practices. *The Reading Teacher, 68*(7), 552–559.

Trumbauer, L. (2004). *All about light*. New York, NY: Scholastic.

VanSledright, B. A. (2002). Fifth graders investigating history in the classroom: Results from a researcher-practitioner design experiment. *The Elementary School Journal, 103*(2), 131–160.

Wiggins, G., & McTighe, J. (2005). *Understanding by design* (2nd ed.). Alexandria, VA: Association for Supervision and Curriculum Development.

Wilson, A. A. (2011). A social semiotics framework for conceptualizing content area literacies. *Journal of Adolescent & Adult Literacy, 54*(6), 435–444.

Wineburg, S. S. (1991). Historical problem solving: A study of the cognitive processes used in the evaluation of documentary and pictorial evidence. *Journal of Educational Psychology, 83*(1), 73–87.

Wineburg, S. (2001). *Historical thinking and other unnatural acts*. Philadelphia, PA: Temple University Press.

Wright, T. S., & Gotwals, A. W. (2017). Supporting disciplinary talk from the start of school: Teaching students to think and talk like scientists. *The Reading Teacher, 71*(2), 189–197.

Yopp, R. H., & Yopp, H. K. (2012). Young children's limited and narrow exposure to informational text. *The Reading Teacher, 65*(7), 480–490.

Young, E. (2016). *Lon Po Po: A Red-Riding Hood story from China*. New York, NY: Puffin Books.

Index

Adair, M., 88, 103
All About Light (Trumbauer), 105–108
Altieri, J. L., 20
Alvermann, D. E., 33, 91
Amanti, C., 37–38
American Association for the Advancement of
  Science, 91
Animated videos, 80, 83, 98, 100
Animoto, 100
Annotation tools/strategy, 49, 63, 72, 74, 95, 121
Anticipation guide strategy, 34, 48, 121
Arazi, J., 142
Artell, M., 54–57, 59, 61–62
Assessment
  backward design (Wiggins & McTighe) and,
    30–31
  digital tools in disciplinary literacy, 22, 30–32,
    56, 60, 80, 83
  in English language arts (ELA), 56, 60
  in mathematics, 80, 83, 85–86
  performance tasks/authentic learning tools in,
    30–31, 34
  in science, 98, 105, 107–108
  in social studies, 129, 132
Audible, 59
Audio recorders/recordings, 49, 59, 63, 76, 83,
  84, 105–109, 110, 121, 130
Audio-supported annotation tools, 74
Avatar tools, 32

Backward design (Wiggins & McTighe), 30–31
Bauer, F. B., 142
Bean, Thomas W., ix–x, 9, 47
Beck, I. L., 17, 121
Beschorner, B., 11, 136–137
BoomWriter, 100
Branch, Mrs., 3, 19–20, 40, 64, 87, 111, 136
Britt, J., 7
Brock, C. H., 6, 10, 20, 33, 112
Broomhead, P., 15
Buelow, S., 14

C3 Framework for Social Studies State Standards
  (NCSS), 16, 112, 113–119, 126
Caparo, M. M., 73
Caparo, R. M., 73

Cappello, M., 91
CAST (Center for Applied Social Technology),
  37, 39
Castek, J., 12–13, 71
CCSS. See Common Core State Standards (CCSS)
  Initiative
Center for Applied Social Technology (CAST),
  37, 39
Chatterpix, 105–109, 110
Civics. See also Social studies
  Core Disciplinary Practice overview, 16
  experts and expert practices, 114, 115, 116
  integrating disciplinary literacy into, 112
Closed questions
  essential questions (EQs) vs., 25–26
  examples of, 26
  nature of, 25
Close reading strategy
  in English language arts (ELA) text analysis,
    47–48
  in mathematics text analysis, 73
  in social sciences, 121
Collaborative class websites, 75
Collaborative conversations strategy, 76
Collaborative digital graphic organizers, 134–135
Collaborative-writing tools, 100
College, Career, and Civic Life (C3) Framework
  for Social Studies State Standards (NCSS), 16,
  112, 113–119, 126
Colwell, Jamie, 7, 10, 11, 13, 27, 28, 45, 70–71,
  92, 119, 139, 143
Common Core State Standards (CCSS) Initiative,
  6–7
  in English language arts (ELA), 40, 42–45,
    53, 59
  in mathematics, 64–65, 67–70, 73–74, 77–78
  in science, 90–91
  in social studies/history, 113–114, 127
Communicating
  in Core Disciplinary Practice, 18
  in English language arts (ELA), 50–51
  in mathematics, 74–76, 78, 86
  in science, 98–100, 102, 110
  in social studies, 122–124
Computer science connection coding apps, 100
Conderman, G., 47

Conradi, K., 13–14
Content-area literacy. *See also* English language arts (ELA); Mathematics; Science; Social studies
disciplinary literacy vs., 2, 7, 8–9
three-phase approach to, 33
Core Disciplinary Practices, 14–18
communication to present disciplinary understanding, 18
in English language arts (ELA), 16, 41–42, 46–51, 52–62
integrating into instruction, 20–21. *See also* Planning Elementary Digitally Supported Disciplinary Literacy (PEDDL) Framework
long-range planning and, 137–139
in mathematics, 16, 65–67, 71–76, 78, 80–82, 86
nature of, 6, 15–18, 20–21
overview by discipline, 16
recognizing/comprehending multiple text types, 17
in science, 16, 89–90, 92, 94–100, 101, 110
in social studies, 16, 113–114, 115, 117–118, 120–124, 125–133
summary of, 15–18
text analysis and critique, 17
vocabulary used in discipline, 18
Council of Chief State School Officers (CCSS), 6–7, 64–65
Culturally responsive disciplinary literacy instruction, 28, 29–30, 45–46, 70–71, 92, 119
Dalton, B., 5, 28
De Lange, J., 65
Deshler, D. D., 9, 33
Digital annotation tools, 49, 63, 74, 95
Digital audio recorders/recordings, 63, 83, 105–109, 110, 121, 130
Digital autobiographies, 49
Digital bookmarking tools, 63
Digital cameras, 124
Digital charts, 49
Digital documents, 121, 123
Digital drawing applications, 75
Digital films, 51
Digital graphic organizers, 34, 48, 50, 72, 75, 121, 130, 131, 134–135
Digital graphing tools, 70
Digital image presentation tools, 100
Digital image repositories, 124
Digital literacies for disciplinary learning
nature of, 12–13
in PEDDL Framework, 22, 30–32
Digitally supported disciplinary literacy. *See also* Digital tools *and specific disciplines*
importance of, 5–6
nature of, 2, 13
in PEDDL Framework, 22, 23, 32–35, 46–51
Digital map creators, 123

Digital resource archives, 121
Digital simulation tools, 95
Digital storyboards, 32, 34, 62, 63
Digital tables, 72
Digital tools
in assessing disciplinary literacy, 22, 30–32, 56, 60, 80, 83
in English language arts (ELA), 42, 43, 46–51, 56–57, 60–62, 63
integration of, 23
introducing new tools to students, 140–141
long-range planning and, 137–139
in mathematics, 66–67, 71–76, 80–81, 82–84, 85–86
nature of, 31, 32–33
in science, 89–90, 95, 96, 98–100, 105–109, 110
in social studies, 114, 116, 121, 123, 124, 129–135
in supporting disciplinary literacy instruction, 22, 32–35
Digital video, 50, 124
Diigo, 63
Directed reading-thinking activity (DRTA), 96
Disciplinary literacy, 5–18
academic language instruction and, 14, 18
applications in grades K–5, 6–8
challenges in K-5 classroom, 1–2, 10–11
connections with content-area literacy, 2, 7, 9
content-area literacy vs., 2, 8–9
Core Disciplinary Practices in. *See* Core Disciplinary Practices
digital tools in. *See* Digital tools
diverse classrooms and, 6, 11
emergence of, 9
in English language arts (ELA). *See* English language arts (ELA)
goals in K-5 classroom, 12
guided retelling and, 14
importance of, 6–7
linkage with English language arts (ELA) in K-5 classroom, 10–11, 27, 40–46, 118–119
in mathematics. *See* Mathematics
nature of, 1, 5–6, 7
nature of "text" in, 9–10, 11, 13–14, 17–18
as a perspective, 20
planning for K–5 classroom, 20–21, 136–144. *See also* Planning Elementary Digitally Supported Disciplinary Literacy (PEDDL) Framework
research on, 13–14
in science. *See* Science
in social studies. *See* Social studies
state and national standards and. *See* Standards
Disciplinary Text Selection Table (Colwell), 28, 29–30
for English language arts (ELA), 29, 45–46
for mathematics, 30, 70–71
for science, 30, 92, 93

for social studies, 29, 119
Diversity/diverse learners
in English language arts (ELA), 57, 62
funds of knowledge (Moll et al.), 37–39
instruction design for all students, 140
in K-5 classrooms, 6, 11
in mathematics, 81, 84–85
in PEDDL Framework, 22, 35–39, 140
in science, 106, 109–110
in social studies, 131, 133
student vs. teacher demographics and, 6
trends in classrooms, 6
Dobler, E., 134
Draper, R. J., 9–10, 15, 45, 64–65, 88, 103
Drew, S. V., 9, 33
Duke, N. K., 17, 27
Dunkerly-Bean, J., 47

Eagleton, M., 134
Economics. See also Social studies
experts and expert practices, 115, 116
integrating disciplinary literacy into, 112–113
Edmodo, 96
Educreations, 74
English language arts (ELA), 40–63
assessment in, 56, 60
communicating in, 50–51
Core Disciplinary Practices, 16, 41–42, 46–51, 52–62
digital tools in, 42, 43, 46–51, 56–57, 60–62, 63
diversity/diverse learners in, 57, 62
experts and expert practices, 16, 41–42, 43
grade 2 sample lesson, 52–62
grade 5 lesson plan template, 63, Online Appendix A
integrating disciplinary literacy into, 40–46
linkage with disciplinary literacy in K-5 classroom, 10–11, 27, 40–46, 118–119
in PEDDL Framework, 52–62
questions to ponder, 63
standards in, 16, 40, 42–45, 53, 59
text analysis, 47–48, 49, 60
text selection, 29, 45–46, 55–59
vocabulary use, 48–50
Essential questions (EQs)
closed questions vs., 25–26
examples of, 26
nature of, 25
in Planning Elementary Digitally Supported Disciplinary Literacy (PEDDL) Framework, 25–27, 31
Estapa, A., 11
Exit slip strategy, 51
Experts
in English language arts (ELA), 16, 41–42, 43
in mathematics, 16, 65–67
in science, 16, 88–91, 93
in social studies, 16, 113–114, 115–116, 123

Faggella-Luby, M. N., 9, 33
Fang, Z., 143
Fishbowl Discussions, 8–9
Fisher, D., 47–48
Fisher, R., 46
Fleener, C. E., 33
Flowers, A. C., 142
Four square strategy, 50
Frambaugh-Kritzer, C., 14
Frayer Model, 75
Freebody, P., 17
Frey, N., 47–48
Funds of knowledge (Moll et al.), 37–38

Gambrell, L., 17
Geography. See also Social studies
Core Disciplinary Practice overview, 16
experts and expert practices, 115, 116
integrating disciplinary literacy into, 113
Gillis, V. R., 33, 47
Glogster, 100
Goatley, V. J., 6, 10, 20, 33
Goldman, S., 143
Goldring, R., 6
Gonzalez, N., 37–38
Google Classroom, 56, 96
Google Docs, 43, 50, 100
Google Drawings, 129, 132
Google Earth, 95
Gotwals, A. W., 7
Grade 1
English language arts (ELA) communication, 51
English language arts (ELA) standards and disciplinary practices, 44
English language arts (ELA) texts, 49
mathematics communication, 76
mathematics standards and disciplinary literacy practices, 68
mathematics texts, 72
mathematics vocabulary instruction, 75
science communication, 100
science sample lesson, 101–110
science standards and disciplinary literacy practices, 92
science texts, 94, 95
social studies texts, 121
social studies vocabulary instruction, 123
Grade 2
English language arts (ELA) sample lesson, 52–62
English language arts (ELA) standards and disciplinary practices, 44
English language arts (ELA) texts, 48
English language arts (ELA) vocabulary instruction, 50
mathematics standards and disciplinary literacy practices, 68
mathematics texts, 74

Grade 2 *(continued)*
  science standards and disciplinary literacy
    practices, 92
  science texts, 96
  science vocabulary instruction, 98
  social studies communication, 124
  social studies standards, 117–118
  social studies texts, 121
Grade 3
  English language arts (ELA) communication, 51
  English language arts (ELA) standards and
    disciplinary practices, 45
  English language arts (ELA) texts, 49
  mathematics communication, 76
  mathematics lesson plan template, 77, 86,
    Online Appendix B
  mathematics standards and disciplinary literacy
    practices, 69
  mathematics texts, 72
  mathematics vocabulary instruction, 75
  science communication, 100
  science standards and disciplinary literacy
    practices, 92
  science texts, 94, 95
  social studies texts, 121
  social studies vocabulary instruction, 123
Grade 4
  English language arts (ELA) standards and
    disciplinary practices, 45
  English language arts (ELA) texts, 48
  English language arts (ELA) vocabulary
    instruction, 50
  mathematics standards and disciplinary literacy
    practices, 69
  mathematics texts, 74
  science lesson plan template, 101, 110, Online
    Appendix C
  science standards and disciplinary literacy
    practices, 93
  science texts, 96
  science vocabulary instruction, 98
  social studies communication, 124
Grade 5
  English language arts (ELA) communication, 51
  English language arts (ELA) lesson plan
    template, 63, Online Appendix A
  English language arts (ELA) standards and
    disciplinary practices, 45
  English language arts (ELA) texts, 49
  mathematics communication, 76
  mathematics standards and disciplinary literacy
    practices, 69
  mathematics texts, 72
  mathematics vocabulary instruction, 75
  science communication, 100
  science standards and disciplinary literacy
    practices, 93
  science texts, 94, 95
  social studies sample lesson, 125–133

social studies standards, 117–118
social studies texts, 121
social studies vocabulary instruction, 123
Graham, A. C. K., 11
Graner, P. S., 9, 33
Graphic organizers/graphic organizer strategy,
  34, 48, 50, 72, 75, 121, 124, 130, 131,
  134–135
Grouping strategy, 48
Guided retelling model (Parenti), 14
Guiding questions, 35

Håland, A., 10–11
Halladay, J. L., 73
Hamilton, R. L., 121
Hart, S. M., 24
Haubner, J. P., 7, 9, 10, 87–88
Hebard, H., 7, 9, 10, 87–88
Hedin, L. R., 47
Herczog, M. M., 113–114
History. *See also* Social studies
  Core Disciplinary Practice overview, 16
  experts and expert practices, 115, 116
  integrating disciplinary literacy into, 112
  in Planning Elementary Digitally Supported
    Disciplinary Literacy (PEDDL) Framework,
    24, 27, 28–29, 32, 33–35, 38–39
  text selection, 29
Horsey, M., 7
House on Maple Street, The (Pryor), 135
Hutchison, Amy C., 11, 13, 23, 27, 28, 63, 71,
  139, 143
Hynd-Shanahan, C., 33, 47

Inquiry-based learning, 7
Inquiry charts strategy, 49
Interactive read-aloud strategy, 50
Interactive topographic maps, 121
Interactive whiteboards, 72, 83
International Literacy Association, 16
Internet news resources, 74

Jensen, A. P., 15
Jigsaw strategy, 95
Johnson, D., 11
Johnson, K., 11
Juel, C., 7, 9, 10, 87–88

Kang, G. Y., 142
Kerkhoff, S. N., 11
Kindergarten
  English language arts (ELA) standards and
    disciplinary literacy practices, 44
  English language arts (ELA) texts, 48
  English language arts (ELA) vocabulary
    instruction, 50
  mathematics sample lesson, 77–85
  mathematics standards and disciplinary literacy
    practices, 68

mathematics texts, 74
science standards and disciplinary literacy
practices, 92
science texts, 96
science vocabulary, 98
social studies communication, 124
social studies lesson plan template, 135, Online
Appendix D
social studies texts, 121
Kinesthetic role play strategy, 124
King, J. R., 24
Kucan, L., 121
KWL (What I Want to Know, What I Know, and
What I Learned) charts, 8–9, 34, 95

Labeling strategy, 48
Ladson-Billings, G., 37
Lafferty, K., 91
Leedy, Loreen, 82–83, 84
Lemke, J. L., 88
Lemley, S. M., 24
Leveled primary source websites, 121
Leveled texts, 46, 55–59, 60–62, 118, 128, 131
Lew, S., 14, 24
Liebfreund, M. D., 13–14
Listing strategy, 48
Little Red Riding Hood (leveled text), 55–57,
59, 60–62
Long-range planning, 136–139
Lon Po Po (Young), 54–57, 59, 61–62
Loxterman, J. A., 17
Luke, A., 17

Maloch, B., 7
Manderino, M., 12–13, 71
Marinak, B., 17
Mathematics, 64–86
assessment in, 80, 83, 85–86
communicating in, 74–76, 78, 86
Core Disciplinary Practices, 16, 65–67, 71–76,
77, 78, 80–82, 86
digital tools in, 66–67, 71–76, 80–81, 82–84,
85–86
diversity/diverse learners in, 81, 84–85
experts and expert practices, 16, 65–67
grade 3 lesson plan template, 77, 86, Online
Appendix B
integrating disciplinary literacy into, 64–71
kindergarten sample lesson, 77–85
in PEDDL Framework, 77–85
questions to ponder, 85–86
standards in, 16, 64–65, 67–70, 73–74, 77–78
text analysis, 73, 74
text selection, 30, 70–72, 80, 82–83
vocabulary use, 73–74, 75, 78, 84
McKeown, M. G., 17, 121
McTighe, J., 25–26, 30–31
McTigue, E. M., 142
Merkley, D., 34

Ming, K., 7
Mission: Addition (Leedy), 80, 82–83, 84
Modeling comprehension strategy, 72
Moje, E. B., 6, 7, 9, 15, 25, 28
Moll, L. C., 37–38
Moore, D. W., 8
Moran, M., 7, 9, 10, 87–88
Morgan, R. F., 33

Nadolny, L., 11
Naraian S., 142
National Center for Education Statistics, 6, 38
National Council for the Social Studies (NCSS),
16, 112, 113–119, 126
National Council of Teachers of English (NCTE),
16
National Council of Teachers of Mathematics
(NCTM), 16, 65–66
National Geographic Kids, 121
National Governors Association Center for Best
Practices (NGACBP), 6–7, 64–65
National Reading Panel, 142
National Research Council, 91
National Science Teacher Association, 91
Nearpod, 72
Neff, C., 37–38
Neumann, M. D., 73
Newsela, 121
Next Generation Science Standards (NGSS) Lead
States, 16, 87, 88–93, 97, 102–103, 104
Nokes, J. D., 24

Obenchain, K. M., 112
Ogle, D. M., 34
Online response tools, 51
Open shape sort strategy, 72

Padlets, 97–99
Paired retelling strategy, 49
Parenti, M., 14
PBS, 128, 131
Peck, S., 7
PEDDL Framework. See Planning Elementary
Digitally Supported Disciplinary Literacy
(PEDDL) Framework
PEDDL Lesson Plan Templates
basic template, 3, 39, Online Appendix E
Elementary Digitally Supported Disciplinary
Literacy Framework overview, 21–22
grade 1 science, 104–106
grade 2 English language arts, 54–57
grade 3 mathematics, 77, 86, Online Appendix B
grade 4 science, 101, 110, Online Appendix C
grade 5 English language arts (ELA), 63,
Online Appendix A
grade 5 social studies, 127–131
kindergarten mathematics, 79–81
kindergarten social studies, 135, Online
Appendix D

Pennington, J. L., 112
Performance tasks/authentic assessment tools,
    30–31, 34
Petite Rouge (Artell), 54–57, 59, 61–62
Phelps, S. F., 33
Picture books, 80, 82–83, 84
Planning Elementary Digitally Supported Disci-
    plinary Literacy (PEDDL) Framework, 19–39
    considerations for diverse learners, 22, 35–39,
        140
    development of, 2–3
    discrepancies in abilities across grades 1-5,
        141–142
    in English language arts (ELA), 52–62
    explicit disciplinary instruction, 142–143
    general ideas for practice, 39
    introducing new digital tools to students,
        140–141
    long-range planning and, 136–139
    in mathematics, 77–85
    overview of, 21–23
    PEDDL Planning Template. *See* PEDDL Lesson
        Plan Templates
    Phase 1: Identifying Appropriate Disciplinary
        Literacy Practices, 21, 23–24, 36, 53, 54,
        77–81, 101–103, 104, 126, 127
    Phase 2: Framing Disciplinary Literacy, 21,
        25–27, 36, 53–58, 79, 81–82, 103, 104,
        126–127, 128
    Phase 3: Selecting Multimodal Texts for
        Disciplinary Literacy, 21, 27–30, 36, 38,
        55, 58–59, 80, 82–83, 105, 107, 128,
        131–132
    Phase 4: Assessing Disciplinary Literacy with a
        Variety of Tools, 22, 30–32, 36, 38, 56, 60,
        80, 83, 105, 129, 132
    Phase 5: Digitally Supporting Disciplinary
        Literacy Instruction, 22, 32–35, 36, 56–57,
        60–62, 81, 83–84, 106, 130, 132–133
    Phase 6: Reflecting to Reach All Learners, 22,
        35–37, 57, 62, 81, 84–85, 106, 131, 133
    professional learning networks (PLNs) and,
        143–144
    sample lesson plans, 52–62, 77–85, 101–110,
        125–133
    in science, 88, 101–110
    in social studies, 24, 27, 28–29, 32, 33–35,
        38–39, 125–133
    time concerns of teachers, 139–140
Podcasts, 51, 95
Popp, J., 143
Possible sentences strategy, 50
Previewing strategy, 48, 95, 121
Professional learning networks (PLNs), 143–144
Promethean Board, 84
Pryor, Bonnie, 135

Questioning the Author strategy, 121, 129, 132,
    133, 134

RAFT Writing strategy, 8–9, 51, 98–99, 100, 124
Rainey, E. C., 16, 41, 50
Raphael, T. E., 6, 10, 20, 33
Readence, J. E., 8
Readers' Theater, 8–9
Reading A-Z, 54–57, 59
Reading the Web (Dobler & Eagleton), 134
Read-write-pair-share strategy, 74
readwritethink.org, 60
Reflection guide strategy, 100
Reinking, D., 23
Response writing strategy, 76
Richardson, J. S., 33
Rickelman, R. J., 8
Rupley, W. H., 73

Sample lessons
    English language arts (ELA, grade 2), 52–62
    mathematics (kindergarten), 77–85
    science (grade 1), 101–110
    social studies (grade 5), 125–133
Schleppegrell, M. J., 143
Schmidt-Crawford, D., 11
Science, 87–110
    assessment in, 98, 105, 107–108
    communicating in, 98–100, 102, 110
    Core Disciplinary Practices, 16, 89–90, 92,
        94–100, 101, 110
    digital tools in, 89–90, 95, 96, 98–100,
        105–109, 110
    diversity/diverse learners in, 106, 109–110
    experts and expert practices, 16, 88–91, 93
    grade 1 sample lesson, 101–110
    grade 4 lesson plan template, 101, 110, Online
        Appendix C
    integrating disciplinary literacy into, 87–94
    in PEDDL Framework, 88, 101–110
    questions to ponder, 110
    standards in, 16, 87, 88–93, 97, 102–103, 104
    text analysis, 94–97
    text selection, 30, 91–94, 105, 107
    vocabulary use, 97–98, 99, 101, 102, 110
Science and Engineering Practices, 97
Scieszka, J., 58–59
ScratchJr, 100
Screencasts, 48, 76
Semantic feature analysis, 123
Shanahan, C., 6, 7, 9–11, 14, 15, 18, 20, 23–24,
    27, 41, 45, 46, 97, 143
Shanahan, T., 6, 7, 9–11, 14, 15, 18, 20, 23–24,
    27, 41, 45, 46, 97, 143
Shareable tables, 74
Shared-reading strategy, 123
Show Me, 83
Siebert, D., 9–10, 15, 45, 64–65
Siffrinn, N., 14, 24
Sinatra, G. M., 17
Smagorinsky, P., 11, 41, 48, 50
Smith, L., 58–59

Index

157

Smithsonian Learning Lab, 130, 131, 133
Social studies, 111–135
  assessment in, 129, 132
  communicating in, 122–124
  Core Disciplinary Practices, 16, 113–114, 115, 117–118, 120–124, 125–133
  digital tools, 114, 116, 121, 123, 124, 129–135
  diversity/diverse learners in, 131, 133
  experts and expert practices, 16, 113–114, 115–116, 123
  grade 5 sample lesson, 125–133
  integrating disciplinary literacy into, 111–120
  kindergarten lesson plan template, 135, Online Appendix D
  in Planning Elementary Digitally Supported Disciplinary Literacy (PEDDL) Framework, 24, 27, 28–29, 32, 33–35, 38–39, 125–133
  questions to ponder, 134–135
  standards in, 16, 112, 113–119, 126, 127
  text analysis, 120–122, 125–126, 128, 135
  text selection, 29, 119–120, 128, 131–132, 134
  vocabulary use, 122, 123
Special education services, 38
Speech-to-text tools, 76
Spires, H. A., 11
Split-page note-taking strategy, 74
Standards, 6–7
  in English language arts (ELA), 16, 40, 42–45, 53, 59
  in mathematics, 16, 64–65, 67–70, 73–74, 77–78
  in science, 16, 87, 88–93, 97, 102–103, 104
  in social studies, 16, 112, 113–119, 126, 127
Steele, J. S., 14
Storyboard, 62
Stromer, E., 11
Study/observe-write-pair-share strategy, 96
Summarizing strategy, 51, 74

Tablets, 72, 74, 76, 96, 97, 99
Taie, S., 6
Taylor, V., 143
Text
  analysis and critique of, 17, 47–48
  in Core Disciplinary Practice, 17
  in disciplinary literacy, 9–10, 11, 13–14, 17–18
  Disciplinary Text Selection Table (Colwell), 28, 29–30, 45–46, 70–71, 92, 93, 119
  for diverse learners, 38
  English language arts (ELA) text selection and analysis, 29, 45–49, 55–59, 60
  mathematics text selection and analysis, 30, 70–74, 80, 82–83

  producing to present disciplinary understanding, 18
  recognizing and comprehending multiple types of, 17
  as scaffold to disciplinary learning, 27–28
  science text selection and analysis, 30, 91–97, 105, 107
  social studies text selection and analysis, 29, 119–122, 125–126, 128, 131–132, 134, 135
Text impressions strategy, 75
Think-aloud strategy, 76, 96
Thinklink, 98
Thoma, J., 11
Three Little Pigs, The, 58–59
Toppel, K., 7, 38
Trost-Shahata, E., 6, 10, 20, 33
True Story of the Three Little Pigs, The (Scieszka & Smith), 58–59
Trumbauer, Lisa, 105–108

VanSledright, B. A., 7, 10
Venn diagrams, 60
Video clips, 48, 50, 80, 83, 96, 98, 100, 124
Video conferencing tools, 50
Video slideshow makers, 76
Virtual reality tools, 95
Visualization strategy, 100
Vocabulary
  academic language instruction and, 14, 18
  in Core Disciplinary Practice, 18
  in English language arts (ELA), 48–50
  in mathematics, 73–74, 75, 78, 84
  in science, 97–98, 99, 101, 102, 110
  in social studies, 122, 123
Vocabulary card strategy, 75
Voice recorders, 72
Voki, 32

Weber, C. M., 6, 10, 20, 33
Whiteboards, 72, 83
Wiggins, G., 25–26, 30–31
Wildwood Elementary School, 19–20. See also Branch, Mrs.
Wilson, A. A., 9, 91
Wineburg, S. S., 24, 112
Woodward, Lindsay, 11, 23, 28, 63, 136–137, 143
Word wall strategy, 75, 97–99, 123
Wright, T. S., 7

Yopp, H. K., 47
Yopp, R. H., 47
Young, E., 54–57, 59, 61–62

About the Authors

Dr. Jamie Colwell is an associate professor and assistant department chair in the Department of Teaching and Learning at Old Dominion University. She researches disciplinary literacy, primarily in preservice and in-service teacher education, and the role digital technology plays in supporting literacy instruction.

Dr. Amy Hutchison is an associate professor and director of the Division of Elementary, Literacy, and Secondary Education at George Mason University. She studies the ways digital technology influences literacy, instruction, and learning innovations and solutions.

Dr. Lindsay Woodward is an assistant professor in the School of Education at Drake University. She researches how students navigate digital spaces and approaches to supporting teachers as they integrate technology into their instruction.